Dear Jacob

SABELO SOWETO MANDLANZI

Order this book online at www.trafford.com
or email orders@trafford.com

Most Trafford titles are also available at major online book retailers.

Printed in the United States of America.

ISBN: 978-1-4669-7867-6 (sc)
ISBN: 978-1-4669-7866-9 (hc)
ISBN: 978-1-4669-7868-3 (e)

Library of Congress Control Number: 2013901724

Trafford rev. 04/05/2013

 www.trafford.com

North America & international
toll-free: 1 888 232 4444 (USA & Canada)
phone: 250 383 6864 ♦ fax: 812 355 4082

Contents

Foreword vii

Author Biography ix

About Author xi

Dedication xiii

Acknowledgements xv

Words from the Author xvii

The Name Jacob 1

The Origin of Jacob 3

Sale of Land 11

Nearby Economic Crisis 13

Let Us Continue Digging Wells 14

Jacob Has the Spy Types 16

Ministers and Public Servants of the State 19

Jacob's Formidable Legal Representative 20

Favoured by People 21

Change of Clothes 23

The Skin of a Goat Kid 24

Where do we get such people 25

Jacob's Goat Kid 27

Jacob Acts upon the Mandate 28

How Much 29

Speed of Service Delivery 30

Change of Tone 31

Jacob Uses God's Name 34

Jacob's Emotional Intelligence 37

The Voice of Jacob 41

Transparency of National Systems.. 42

Blessed to Be Served.. 44

Plot Against Jacob... 46

Accountability.. 48

Jacob Is Elected to Save the Future at Stake................................. 49

Jacob Displays an African Value... 53

Jacob: Away from the Home Country 56

"Awuleth' Umshin Wam".. 58

The Stone on the Head..61

The Dream of Jacob 63

The People of the East.. 66

The Three Groups of Flock.. 68

Jacob's One-Minded Leaders... 70

People-First-Based Leadership 72

Jacob Meets Her...74

Jacob and Polygamy 76

Reuben Has Mandrakes 78

Women's Great Role in Leadership... 81

Jacob's Journey Back to Nkandla 83

The Spotted and Black Sheep 86

Effect of Wages to the Economy.. 89

Challenged by Brother 91

Jacob's Charges 95

Support from a Higher Leader 98

Jacob's Strength of Humility... 100

Misalignment in One Body... 104

Your Name Is Not Jacob 105

Jacob and Motlanthe Hug... 106

No to Violence Against Women 108

Reconciliation 110

Circumcision...112

Control of Authority 114

Jacob Repositions Himself...116

You Are Who and What God Says You Are 118

Death of a Leader... 120

Joseph Has a Dream... 123

Jacob Zuma Appoints His Successor 125

Jacob Gathers Them All Babize Bonke Nxamalala 128

The Seat of Legends.. 132

Foreword

WE ARE GRATEFUL to Godfrey Sabelo Mandlanzi (GSM) for updating and reminding us that the Bible is as contemporary as the morning news. It is true that the purpose of every chapter in the Bible is to give the Nations a message that GOD's word lives today with us irrespective of the state of our consciousness of its message as relating to us as individuals.

The seemingly 'old head' on 'young shoulders' in the person of GSM has endeavored to illustrate this to us making a practical example of a historical event manifesting itself in our decade in the African National Congress of South Africa and the present Leader: the Hon JG Zuma; also the President for the Republic of South Africa—2009-2013, and possibly beyond?

GSM's work in this book requires a dedication and commitment to studying and understanding the Bible; the flow of its message and the involvement of GOD in the history of mankind regardless of race, color, or creed. GSM has carefully titled chapters to capture the interest of each intending reader; but committing oneself only to them shall also limit one's spiritual growth. It would be interesting if the readers would seek to understand the Bible truths which at times are embodied in: 'WHAT IS IN THE (PERSON'S) NAME?'

The message of the GOD of Abraham, Isaac, and Jacob, as found in the HOLY BIBLE is the total answer to man's total need of guidance and direction.

I thank you great son!

Mandlezulu Seth Mntaka

Author Biography
By Older Brother

Sabelo was born in the mid 80's in Vryheid Coronation. His first three years on planet earth attested the purpose of God about his life because he lived to see Dr's every night, I have not seen someone young that sick and recovering, his recovery at the age of four gives birth to a poignant moment as Dad "Soweto Sr' passes away, the twilight came too early.

In 1991 he started his education journey when he was registered in a pre primary school located in Cliffdale, there were lot of Indians, but due to financial difficulties Mom faced, she had to take him to a cheaper public school. He started his second education phase in a Primary called Thakazela, at this stage he was known for following the older and the wiser, they called him Mbanjwana because you could see his ribs, he was really thin.

1998 he joined KwaNotshelwa high School for grade eight, then it was standard six. The face of the earth seemed to take its attention towards him, he gained popularity after his love for Sisqo. We thought the boy had finalised a Kwaito deal in 2002 but he said the old him was dead, so he became a born again Christian. It was just another occasion to see what could become of this but the tables turned around, a few folks of his age and his former girlfriends (I hope

Momma does not hear about this, but yes ladies loved this lad) were also saved following his decision.

In 2003 then he started his tertiary education and furthered his studies to the Bachelor Information Systems, completing also the Internal Auditing Training programme and General Internal Auditing. I cannot say we have wasted funds for taking him to varsity but I can assure you that the boy has a different calling, auditing is a limitation of his talents.

In 2010 and 2011 we thought greatness was leaving earth but he survived the odds.

He then published his first book Just Teething For A New Thing in 2012, and now? I am speechless, the boy is limitless let's wait and see but we will all desire to read his Biography if it should be published as a book in the years to come.

Langelihle S Mandlanzi—Big brother.

About Author

By Friends

I HAVE ALWAYS known that Sabelo Godfrey Mandlanzi is a man of many talents however I never thought that he was such a great writer! He could have been a great dancer, soccer player, athlete, model, etc. I mean these are some of the things that he killed when we grew up. It is true though that some talents do mature in and with us. As a young man he was always in spot light and what was confusing to many people was that in the mist of all that he was also doing great at school.

Looking back to 1994 when I met this young man at Coronation, Vryheid, there are a few things I noticed about him but his desire to become a better person was more eminent. What makes me more proud about you is the fact that you didn't feel ashamed of yourself due to the fact that you come from the dusty streets of Coronation but you went on to put together a piece about the first citizen of the country! I really do admire that, especially considering that this is just your second book to be published.

Nkosikhona Mbatha

It has been more than 7 years I met Sabelo. All I have lived to see through his eyes is a dream. Although he enjoys an environment where there are jokes, I have seen him living and dying but still he emerged stronger against the storms of life.

Sabelo you are a role model. There is so much one can say about you, I see you excelling and achieving great success. We have found a friend among us who will not only influence the South Africans but the world as a whole. Wishing and praying that the best may come into your life.

Victor Khanyi

The first time I met Sabelo "Soweto' Mandlanzi as a new recruit to Ngubane & Co I could see that there was a lot of potential within this young lion. Sabelo is one of those rare species with respect at his age. I knew him as our future "TD Jakes" but writing books never crossed my mind. But if you have been blessed with a talent of writing scriptures and preaching on a daily basis I guess writing a book will be less of your worries. Usually I tease him by referring to him as Pastor even now. The way he addresses people is out of this world. A man who will not fear to challenge the way we think about social issues.

Being a motivational speaker is not for everyone but Sabelo is gifted in that field as well. He is a good example to the youth of today that you don't have to be raised from presidential palace in order to achieve your dreams. I never thought one day he will be writing a book about our current President for the Republic, President Jacob Zuma, this may take his artist work to another level. He never stops surprising me and with that I will forever respect you. I salute you Sabelo and don't look back and keep it up the great work. You are a true inspiration.

Mlungisi Ncwane

Dedication

My parents

- Although I would have loved to meet Soweto Sr. (my late dad),
  my mom is the queen of my soul, Macingwane. Mntungwa
  Mashobane Mzilikazi, you are a father to me, not a stepfather.

My siblings—Mandlanzi Mad-Love Firm

- You are my blood in special vessels. Ms. Xoli, this is jam bread,
  not jam one. Langelihle Giza, you are the main geyser of the
  house. Zamo, you are bigger than New York City in my heart!
  Sneh Mshanam'-Ndabezitha Mageba Mtwana, I carry you in
  my thoughts. Kuhle, you are a rocket of a troop, and Siphesihle
  Khumalo, imagine the sky; I will be your jet.

God's Purpose Church

- It's like I am letting you down lately since I have twirled my
  focus. I owe you a complete Bible-based service, and when I
  should come back again, I will wash your feet because your
  smiles and prayers are my great might in every protracted mile.

My Forever-Present Mentor, Seth Mandlezulu Mntaka

- Could I ever meet the criteria of rest ("Rest is change of duty.")?

To all my friends, I simply want to thank you for the pivotal role you have played in my makings. Let's set a straight and unbreakable record.

Acknowledgements

Ms. Pam Rehman, you are a timeless wo-man-ager. If that is what we achieved through the *Just Teething* book launch, just imagine what we could accomplish in 2013.

DEAR JACOB G. ZUMA, MEET JACOB S. Mandlanzi, the Invincible, Incredible, Immortal

Words from the Author

A LAD WAS I when they said to me the world was flat and if I journeyed without pause, I would eventually fall in a hole where I might be indiscernible. My inner faculties were subsequently imprisoned by pathetic limitations of restricted human insight. Though we kneeled and milked my uncle's cows in Danny Dalton, it was as if I were destined to be a car mechanic. While I milked Jamludi, I imagined an engine of a sophisticated car. The scars and the tears of the years failed to stop me from dreaming. Bit by bit, dreaming was making me whole.

I longed to discover the end of a man who steps beyond the margin of his strength during his mission; will he crack or become an emblem of victory? My aim grew bigger than attaining fame. I am therefore going to empty every gift on my name in order to serve this generation. Mr. *Just Teething for a New Thing* is my first stride to the great beginnings my spirit wordlessly anticipates, even to this hour.

Photo by Zaba Ngubane, Logoman

My impromptu visit to Nkandla narrowed my space to nurse my cynicism. That was the place where I learned how to face stubborn opposition without help. The sound of a punch was enough to expose cowards; here you saw how a face drastically changed its shape—*bang!* It was the hit of a fist. Although I had inner fears because of the size of my opponent, I could not show that through my face; it would have become his ace card. Life is like a race sometimes. The worse fight is invisible; therefore, we shoved each other with shoulders as if we were soldiers. We threw nerve-racking words against each other; each word became a key determinant to the loss or success of the fight. I am still shocked how one overcame such nights with words.

Ever since words gave light to my heart, the all-encompassing meaning of *Jacob lighted up my* nights, Jacob became a passage of a greater purpose, and this made Jacob to become dear to God and those who realised that his whole life was like a boat, a method in which a nation accomplished transition. Therefore this volume is the equivalent of modern truism that history merely repeats itself, but history is not always a chest of worst incidents, as the connotation may subconsciously induce itself from a negative perspective, sometimes it is a trip from the worst to the best things in life.

The President of the Republic of South Africa,
Union Buildings,
Private Bag X1000,
Pretoria
0001

Dear Jacob G. Zuma,

Your Excellency, I am humbled beyond measure to be entrusted with such an opportunity not only to write this letter and narrate such a realistic anecdote but just to be the least means of communication for a heavenly perspective in such a deafening era. Furthermore, it humbles me to foretell such good tidings, for I am much smaller to wear the sandals of the great prophets of God who saved the race in the day of God's anger, the likes of Elijah, Isaiah, Jeremiah, and Daniel; the list is endless, but we have found limitless grace even more than they did, so blessed is this day, I still say.

Though I had so much unease in tackling this notion, it is as intense as carrying the fate of this generation in one revelation. I went through much elevation in my spirit from the time I audaciously inscribed every vision into this manuscript just as I saw and heard it.

As a black child, I was taught to never look at my elders in their eyes; therefore, I wrote on the ground with my toe, my head bowed, so my face looked down.

I turned out to be inquisitive as the story was uncovered to me, and it became harder to oppose the connotations therein. I found each event relevant; consequently, I could not pretend as if I did not see the relationship between Jacob and His Excellency. It is such connection that has become a significant component of this letter. Progressively, I found your experiences in his circumstances, and my knees shook because I feared that some well-esteemed deacons would suppose such idea to have no reverence for the foundation of Christianity. Well, it is the politics of Babylon that became Daniel's radiance.

In this ephemeral period of my life, I have confirmed frequent tendencies where a meaning of a name persistently haunts a person. If not so, there is a guaranteed level of propensity to follow a name. I imitated a biomedical student by selecting various names as formulae for this experiment, but no matter what name I picked, the result of the analysis broke limits in that Jacob's events and Jacob Zuma's life would not divorce each other from the start to the last part.

Hardly a mirror can keep the reflection of a person when that person is no longer facing the mirror. This is the reason why I assert not His Excellency as Jacob, the son of Isaac. What separates the two mirrors is the time factor, but the reflections are identical twins. Some people live the best and worse years without discovering a glimpse of their fate, yet here, there are acceptable pieces of a puzzle on the floor. Without further ado, may I have a word with you so I may lay bare my revelation?

The Name Jacob

THE NAME JACOB refers to the one who holds a heel.

This meaning jets up a desire to hunt for the person who first owned this name. In every name, there is a special character or personality attached, but who else can then be the person in your name except yourself? Such understanding coerces me to rummage around not only the origin of a name but the persona in the name (i.e., Christ is the person of Jesus). Do folks ever consider the substance of the name Gedleyihlekisa?

The banquet here has assorted desserts, yet I consistently hit upon a book that could be paradoxical to those who look at it; I look after it. The search on biblical records locates a man by the name of Jacob, but who was Jacob, and how does his life become a constructive particle in this search? It is his life, his qualities, that takes the steering wheel; it glues my pen onto the paper.

According to the Book of Life

In Genesis, Abraham begot Isaac, and Isaac begot *Jacob*, and Jacob begot Judah and his brothers. In Matthew, Matthan begot Jacob, and Jacob begot Joseph, the husband of Mary, but this is off course, another Jacob.

This family tree portrays the foundation of the genealogy of Jacob, one of the most blessed genealogies to ever have touched this ground. Though Jacob's life and choices are questionable, what amazes me constantly is realising that he formed part of the foundation of a truly blessed house, from which all those who believe shall also be blessed. Picture this genealogy as the Luthuli House. Abraham, Isaac, and Jacob—do we not have our own? I speak through the eyes of the political struggle. Most leaders who came from the Luthuli House are cherished.

It has been a few years ago. I kept all the coins in a two-litre container during the days when my wallet was undressed and the distance to the restaurant was protracted. I picked up the container to take a rand from it and instantly saw one with a little rust on it; I closed the door lest my search cause noise. I faced it down until all the coins were out, yet when all the coins were on the floor, I still searched for the one coin I had seen. I purged away all the coins to get to it because I basically chose it over the others.

The predicament about being chosen is that there are always many coins in the bucket. Ultimately, they may be newer and even finer until they crowd the chosen coin, but destiny purges its way through to the one. It proves that life isn't just about the assignment. It is more about the relationship between the one who assigns and the assignee. If it were not so, then South Africa would have more than fifty million kingdoms where each man gets to govern. Somebody must be chosen! Will he be perfect and immune against flaws inherent to the human race? The coin had rust; I need to admit that. Most often, limitations and tarnish are a technique of destiny, whose might is unrestricted.

In this Abrahamic family tree, we discover two Jacobs just as I found many coins in the container, but there is a specific Jacob we are looking for, and we won't pick others until we find the one.

The first Jacob is the son of Isaac; perpetually he appears in President Jacob Zuma's mirror as if it were his. Do I want to suggest reincarnation? Certainly not! But my revelation has indications of predestination.

The Origin of Jacob

When the last days of Jacob's grandfather approached, he left *all* he had with his son but gave gifts to the sons of the concubines and sent them away from Isaac. In this way, Isaac found plenty of space to grow big in the land. When Abraham died, Isaac and Ishmael, his sons, buried him in the field he purchased, and there, also, his wife was buried.

Jacob's grandfather was exceedingly blessed. In our day, it is generally hard to find space to bury the dead, but Abraham acquired enough land so that his son would have as much as necessary to build, sow, and develop. This characterizes a victorious blessing because the grandson benefitted from a decision made by his grandfather.

It is, however, a diminutive edition of Abraham's life on earth. Nevertheless, numerous challenges existed between Isaac and Ishmael, the son whom he begot from a maid. This gave birth to opposition and fights over rulership issues. It seemed that the two boys predominantly didn't see eye to eye principally because they shared a father but had different mothers.

Abraham then blessed Isaac before he died, so God blessed Isaac. This clearly displayed the great might of a predecessor's blessing upon the life of a successor. However, God exceptionally omitted this facet if a predecessor stood in the way of a blessed successor.

For this reason, *God chose David even though his father wasn't fond of him during their Mangaung version.* These were practically elections of the next king, who in this day is the figure of a president. Jesse, the father nominated all his sons except David, for he looked at David as a family infamy, therefore he sent David to look after the sheep. But through that rejection, David found divine connection.

A dire situation finds life and motivation for a chosen man.

Critics point more fingers and weaknesses towards David. They say he killed and lacked self-control towards women, yet this slipped them off.

God's selection is final even when there are many cynical fingers upon his preference.

In contrast to the life of Isaac, who is the predecessor of Jacob, we do not find much relevancy about Ishmael. He lived and died because he progressed to diminish, but Isaac had significant descendants because he himself was a destined descendant. Thus, he begot a predestined successor that is none other than Jacob. When Isaac turned forty, he met a gorgeous woman named Rebekah. She was a sister to a man named Laban.

It seemed that, once again, the generational cockroach had found its way to the milk. Abraham waited many years to obtain his promised son. In the same situation, Isaac also waited for almost twenty years with no luck as Rebekah was barren.

Isaac prayed greatly to the Lord for his wife, and the Lord granted his prayer. Rebekah conceived. Generally women are known as spiritual intercessors and prayerful partners, but there is something about a praying leader. I just can't write it down so easily, nevertheless there is time in the spirit where challenges necessitate a prayerful man.

All these men in the bible were human, but when they prayed, God listened and it rained from a cloud as little as a fist of man. Only if men could be prayerful husbands and tame their families, the economy of South Africa would dance as if a new band played a new song, because when a man prays, the nation conceives.

Rebekah portrays South Africa, Abraham represents a strong South African leader, picture the Honourable Nelson Mandela. Barrenness speaks of a time during which black South Africans were oppressed and did not enjoy their stay in this country. Their pain was as the pain of a wife who suffered violence in the house of her father.

You will recall that, for many years, Abraham's wife was barren, and this crisis bridged its way to his son. Abraham waits more years than Isaac to have his first legitimate son, in the same way the generation of the Honourable Nelson Mandela almost equally dealt with the racial-discrimination struggle. It really took them some time and effort. Abraham waited in the prison of barrenness in hope that one day he will have his son and also our political predecessors were imprisoned because of their hope and liberation aspirations.

Barrenness became an opportunity for Isaac. His headship assumed a responsibility to discontinue this deprivation lest it fall unto his successor. This proves though that rulership always has a fair share of intrinsic weaknesses and sufferings. Its package has power and problems.

Generational tendencies that pass from predecessors to successors

God displayed his power towards the prayer of a man; he answered Isaac. Yet a bigger problem began when Isaac's wife conceived. She had twins, and the *two children* struggled together within her to the point that she complained. Two nations were in her womb; two people that shall be separated from her body. One shall be stronger than the other, and *the older* shall *serve the younger*. Since Jacob takes the shadow of Jacob Zuma this foretold us therefore that Jacob Zuma will be president over his predecessor. Generally not all second born sons, deputies and assistants turn out to take the first position. There must be a mighty hand upon the second person.

Why is it that Rebekah complains if she wanted a child? It is because the people of South Africa would also complain about their leaders, the politics of South Africa and pace of delivery of services yet in the first place it is them who voted.

For the first time, there were twins, and the twins fought in the womb. What could this be? The womb represents African National Congress five yearly elections of a president; the contention in Rebekah's womb was prophetic to the contention that would occur when Jacob Zuma challenged former president Thabo Mbeki for presidency.

Dilemma is created by the birth of two leaders; it causes friction between people. The fight that took place before Rebekah gave birth characterized the political convolution that occurred prior to Jacob Zuma taking over as the president of the Republic of South Africa. Much tension was witnessed in Polokwane.

Photo by Gallo Images:. It shows Thabo Mbeki as the president
of the country and Jacob Zuma as the president of the ANC.
Similar to the tension that happened between
Esau and Jacob in Rebekah's womb.

Typically, fathers cherish the birth of sons more than they cherish the birth of a daughter. Sons are a version of their fathers and the vision of the house. They carry upon themselves the surname of the house to the next generation, from one generation to the other. If sons, therefore, symbolize a vision, how shall we have two visions and visionaries in one locality? Two bulls certainly won't make it in one little kraal—remember, Jacob had a twin.

People found themselves in a position where they had to acknowledge two contenders who were both hoping to rule one land. The dawn of a predicament: Jacob wanted to be the president of the house of his father yet not of the nation, but can one be the president of the ANC and not of the country? Jacob's ambitions were a trigger of a Pump gun.

His brother came first and had a right to rule the house and the nation, but Jacob's impatient persistence proves to be a strong force; he is willing to challenge his older brother. But this is no different from the time when Jacob Zuma challenged the honourable former president of the country, Mr. Thabo Mbeki. In 2007, Jacob Zuma sat next to the honourable former president Thabo Mbeki in Polokwane (this was a womb of the country), and they battled for presidency as the two twins fought in Rebekah's womb. What ends this great brotherhood between Jacob and Esau seems to be similar to what ended the beautiful friendship between Jacob Zuma and Thabo Mbeki. Jacob felt that he was stopped to be the one otherwise he could have come out first, but also Thabo Mbeki proposed a commission of enquiry about suspicions of a political plot to block Jacob Zuma to presidency.

A photo by Gallo Images. It displays a conflict between political
twins—Jacob Zuma as Jacob and Thabo Mbeki as Esau.
Interestingly enough, there is Naledi Pandor, former minister of Home
Affairs, who has nothing to do with this analysis, but her presence in
the photo at the back of the two twins is symbolic to the role women
would play in Jacob Zuma's victory, equally to Rebekah's role.

When the time for giving birth arrived, look, there were twins in
her womb. The first one came out red all over, like a hairy garment,
and they called him Esau, for he was hairy, and Jacob held his brother's
heel.

Esau's outward description reflects the qualities of a political
challenger, a person with strong confidence muscles because his
external conditions are extremely interesting and unwrapped to the
public eye. He has the constituents that people often look for when
they want a leader. The fact that Esau was red, which is a different
colour, suggests that Jacob Zuma's secondary opposition would be led
by a leader of different skin colour or race, and as such, we have Helen
Zille, the leader of South Africa's opposition Democratic Alliance
political party in the picture.

Red is bright; women believe it is generally worn by very self-
assured individuals. The whole description proves Esau as an eloquent,
outgoing, and educated leader, but wait until the opposite of that
comes out.

Jacob comes out. I can't imagine the heaviness of the pressure he had to deal with. By virtue of being the second one, he has to prove his capabilities, and there he held his brother's heel, and this took the attention of his parents. Jacob Zuma, being the one who succeeded Thabo Mbeki, somehow also managed to take all the attention even though he lived under the pressure of having to prove himself to those who did not support him.

It is hard to picture a new-born baby *holding something*, let alone *a heel*, but this act foretells about Jacob Zuma's determination to fight through against the odds. It would cost more than a rand to understand this if we opted to hear it from a biological expert. At this age, Jacob had no strength to hold his brother's heel, but this was a version of the judgement some people had before 2008; they underestimated Jacob Zuma's political strength, that he could possibly upset Thabo Mbeki's supporters. When a child is born, her hands are closed, it is believed that there is something she is holding in her hands, her dreams, the future or the gifts of her life, but Jacob was holding his brother's heel, but also when leaders take presidency, they are celebrated, what is the cause of such tension when President Jacob Zuma took over, was he also holding the heel of his brother like Jacob?

This war in the absence of the public confirmed the amount of fight Jacob would have to stomach after birth, but what do see we when Jacob Zuma becomes president? Nothing but blows from the opposition. But since Jacob was willing to take on a bigger fight for what he believed in from birth, Jacob Zuma also took on presidency, which I regard as birth of a new thing. Who had known that, at this stage, one man from the loins of KwaZulu will be a president of this age? This became a new thing, but the new thing had a fight.

His brother's heel is a symbolization of sturdy events in which some brothers would turn their backs against Jacob Zuma. One can't see a person's heel until he has literally turned his back on you. Because of this, many people turned their backs on Jacob Zuma.

*Photo by Gallo Images: Minister of Sports Fikile Mbalula and
President Jacob G Zuma, the two were known to be amathe nolimi
(very close friends), but has Fikile shown Jacob Zuma his heel?*

Sale of Land

At their tender age, the older brother became a cunning hunter, a man of the open country. He basically favoured the world. Jacob was a quiet man who dwelled in the house (tents). This propelled Rebekah's devotion towards Jacob even more. Who is Rebekah? Rebekah is an enormous group of people whose support is propelled by the lack of sympathy thrown at Jacob Zuma.

The interest and attention of Esau and Jacob enlighten us of the variety of issues they would be dealing with if we placed them into this current age. The older one had more influence and interest in the international affairs because he was a man of the open country. Jacob was dominant inside the country because he was a domestic man.

The use of words *open country* may roughly be translated as a focus on international affairs and strong business relationship with other countries. His focus predicts his fate because, though he will do so much, in politics, a leader must be in touch with his people.

Jacob stayed in touch with Rebekah just as Jacob Zuma is in touch with his countless supporters.

When Esau could not catch a game in the open country, he resolved to go back home. This way back home is a direct metaphor of a leader who has spent more time outside the borders of South Africa. When he came back, he was hungry, but this hunger achieves no meaning to this present era if we look at it with blue eyes. His hunger is a representation of desire to govern the home country; therefore, Jacob uses his weakness as an opportunity.

Esau sold his birthright for stew because of hunger. For some of us who recognize the components of a birthright, we know that a major portion of inheritance is land.

The sale of a birthright for stew is a representation of issues that South Africa has to deal with in the expropriation and proper distribution of land. The problem is with officials who trade land in thought of their stomachs. Revered individuals have been associated with cases of obtaining and selling land illegally.

The decision by the government to focus on proper land redistribution is a commendable resolution because it gives us an impression that we are going the Jacob way, which is to regain and control more land instead of selling it to foreigners. Jacob lived in a day where he saw his brother selling his inheritance. This was just a shadow of the problems Jacob Zuma's leadership would face on the topic of land, which is, in fact, the inheritance of generations to be born in South Africa. We have heard that people strive to repossess the land of their forefathers, particularly those who are from the bucolic places, but the early morning open discussions and clear plans the leadership of President Jacob Zuma has unwrapped to the public prove how the government of his Excellency is willing to overcome issues pertaining to land. Your Excellency this is laudable.

Nearby Economic Crisis

THE LIFE OF Jacob has three significant generations: Abraham's, Isaac's, and his generation, yet one of the most similar things they have in common is having to deal with famine.

In actual sense, famine is a personification of an economic and financial crisis, like recession. Since the beginning of time, the world has survived diverse financial crisis. Recession is such a testing time for all leaders because they have to devise strategies to create stability during economical fluctuations. These generations went through this hard time, but their key is how they heeded God's instruction.

God's instruction is the solution

I am a hopeful and positive citizen who believes that we have not reached the dead end; it is a financial bend that necessitates all of us to fasten our belts. I do encourage you, therefore, Mr. President—and your administration—to take South Africa to a much more emergent economy with the equal fortitude of optimism you have delivered. There should be a time when our storeroom has no more room for the crop of the future, and even those taxi commuters choked by tax can eventually get to relax.

In 2009, you were greeted by unbearable global economic recession in your operation to awaken the lives of ordinary citizens, but you did not keep your head down; therefore, not then, and not now.

Let Us Continue Digging Wells

THE TIME BETWEEN the duration of the leadership of Jacob's grandfather and the period of the famine that attacked the land while Isaac lived was long. The earth had faced floods and wars, which closed the wells that had been dug by Jacob's grandfather.

Isaac embarked on a mission to redig all the wells his father dug; these are the same wells their enemies had stopped when they filled the earth.

Isaac's government judiciously opted to dig wells where they could have initiated policies and strategies to afford the preservation of water. I see wells as robust systems in South Africa that are able to create and fulfil the needs of the people. The bet with wells is that we never have to give people water; we dig them a well, and they fetch the water. South Africa is a water scarce country, and water should be used sparingly, in order to preserve it for the generations to come. Your government, His Excellency should be commended in becoming a vehicle to create an awareness of this scarce resource.

The undertaking to achieve five million jobs by 2020 through the infrastructural project plan is more than a proof that your efforts are in line with Isaac's policy.

Jobs are actually in line with this scriptural notion; the county needs firms with job opportunities and other educational and developmental programs that enable citizens to fetch water in its relevant form. Social grants are very commendable, but in time, more citizens will be lethargic if we fail to dig more wells.

Public based investments are commendable especially for those citizens who realize education and information communication technology as the future of the country. It is good to dig such wells because some cisterns cannot hold water. Jeremiah 2:13(b)

Jacob Has the Spy Types

TIME MOVED INCESSANTLY with no ending, and the two brothers, Jacob and Esau, grew even older before their father. The family eventually found a place and settled. Jacob was still ambivalent, but at forty, his brother married the daughters of the daughter of his father's enemies, and this grieved his parents as they realised how much effort they had put into the struggle to make things better for them, and now, it seemed to be all worthless. This was a terrible pain for them, except the fact that they were old. No wound exceeds the pain successors induce when they choose a path that does not honour the founding efforts of the selfless struggle. But the relevant meaning of marriage was still a shadow for the contemporary time. In the essence of this context, this foretold about the sons of the ANC who would have political relationships with opposition parties—to fulfil the words "marry other women"—but often the scripture places *woman* if it refers to a weaker vessel. 1 Peter 3:7

For this reason the African National Congress has remained stronger whether we like it or not because a man must be stronger than a woman, a man must produce sons and sons are heirs, heirs of the inheritance of the land of their fathers. Sons want to take control of the inheritance left by their fathers hence the words "Amandla? Awethu!" have not left the mouth of the ANC

Isaac was surely getting older; his eyes were dim, so he could not see clearly. One day, he called Esau, his eldest son. My son, go and hunt a game for me so that I may bless you." In this context, Isaac was saying, "I will vote for you if you deliver your services.

The statement "his eyes were getting dim" typifies a leader whose strength in relation to the national vision is weakening because of age. Now he is an old man, and legs cannot allow him to run for the country any longer.

This request has more to it than just hunting. Accounts prove beyond doubt that Isaac wanted to bless or vote for Esau, but he had developed the entire leadership framework. He had to be the first one to follow it so that his sons would also regard it. He knew that a blessing had to be tagged along to the one who has performed a service. A different shift would be controversial, but the price of debate was not something he could take at this stage in his life; therefore, Isaac had to stick to the principle of service delivery and democracy. At that time, it meant the predecessor would allow God to intervene in choosing a successive leader over his own personal preference, but we should also have leaders chosen by the people. Isaac favoured Esau, Rebekah favoured Jacob. For a moment, Isaac personifies the anti-Zuma crowd, but there is a cause for Rebekah to support Jacob, she embodies the people and at the moment people support President Jacob Zuma.

But again any leader who can serve his predecessor can serve his nation. Jacob, being the one who undeserved his predecessor's vote, used the system to unlock his fate. Not only did he serve his father but his speed of service delivery became key to his victory. Esau had the right to be blessed, but Jacob was blessed because he served with speed.

While blessing or voting for Esau would fashion conflict and depict autocracy from the old man, their conversation happened in a private room, where Jacob had no chance of finding out about it, but Jacob had a spy inside the house.

Isaac and Esau did not know that Rebekah was slyly listening to the entire conversation, and as Esau left for the open country to hunt for the game, Rebekah quickly took the conversation and told Jacob about it.

Who is Rebekah in this context?

She is a Zuma anonymous who gets the conversation and tapes of the conversation for Jacob Zuma. But since Jacob had a spy, we can confirm that the tapes were later handed to Jacob Zuma. So it's either we say both Jacob and President Jacob Zuma had spies or they both had spy tapes of the conversation they shouldn't have heard from the initial plan of their rivals. Jacob's tapes ultimately restructured his fate.

The spy tapes could only follow Jacob's footsteps.

Ministers and Public Servants of the State

"Now I beseech you, therefore, obey my voice and go now not to the open country but to the flock outside and bring me two good goat kids," said Rebekah.

Rebekah became an agent of change, a proactive servant between the leader and the people, but is this not what the public has sought for?

Leadership officials who turn government policies into action.

There were challenges against Rebekah's conviction, such as the lack of sufficient resources, but her purpose was concrete. There is a great call for the ministers and public servants; Rebekah's audacity should be a motivation against lack of resources in this country. If there is a need to identify the strength of the leadership chain, these are the individuals who form a strong link of the government chain. If it were possible, there would be no flaws identified or prevailing within those sectors that are vehicles of the services of the state, but some institutions have bettered their quality lately, typically a stain always takes the attention on a white coat, but the truth should be shared, at this time there are innumerable positive and progressive things with our motherland. Let us look from place to place, except from the news today and realise how much goodness we have.

Jacob's Formidable Legal Representative

"MOM, MY BROTHER is a hairy man, and you know that I am not a hairy man." Jacob compares himself to Esau with fear that if he should be caught, it would get him into a serious problem, but Rebekah says, "It is fine, Jacob. Let your curse be upon me this time. Go and fetch the goat kids."

Jacob finally found relief and an opportunity to carry his mission without considering the entirety of his issues or that which could happen during his mission. Rebekah here wore a legal hat, now she represents a team of people who are willing to do everything they can to lawfully defend Jacob Zuma on charges laid against him. She said what only strong and formidable legal representatives could say, "I will take it on to me." Hence, it is believed that Jacob had a strong and formidable legal representative, but this is the similar view about Jacob Zuma's team of lawyers and attorneys.

Favoured by People

T HIS ASSIGNMENT WAS not simple, but Rebekah's support gave Jacob much confidence. Consider that this was what Jacob had fought for from birth; this last round of the fight wasn't going to be a dissuasion, so Jacob went and brought the two goat kids, and Rebekah *made the tasty meat.*

Rebekah hastened; time was running out. Quickly she took the best clothes of her eldest son, which were with her, and she put them on Jacob. In such an atmosphere, the tension of fear is likely to become solid! But how is the support of Rebekah different from the support people have given Jacob Zuma?

A photo by Gallo Images that shows Jacob Zuma and his supporters at the back just as Rebekah backed Jacob.

Anyway, Rebekah quickly changed Jacob's clothes and put on him the skins of a goat kid.

What could be the meaning hidden behind Rebekah's decision to take someone else's clothes and give them to Jacob? Esau represents the opposition. This is literally a change of people's votes. Those who voted for other political parties will eventually choose to vote the ANC even though, initially, they were not ANC members, but for Jacob Zuma they will, and this was evidenced when Jacob Zuma won the presidency. In 2009 some IFP members confessed to have voted for the ANC because of President Jacob Zuma, continuously President Jacob Zuma won voluminous votes to the ANC.

Just as Jacob wore his brother's clothes, Jacob Zuma also pocketed Dr Mangosuthu Buthelezi's votes through his admirable charms and the fundamental preceding involvement in the raw political conflict which occurred in KwaZulu Natal, but one could say, primarily these were not Jacob Zuma's votes, should I say those weren't Jacob's clothes?

Change of Clothes

W<small>E WOKE UP</small> so early. It was a Sunday morning; we prepared for church. Not only did we bathe but we changed our clothes. Although church was far, we didn't feel that distance when we took on our new outfits, and somehow, because of the outfits—*the renewal of image*—the journey was shortened.

Therefore, the meaning of the changing of clothes is an important component to understand. Rebekah did not substitute Jacob with Esau—which is also a form of change—but there was a need to change clothes and not the person. Leaders must also realise a need to make the image germane to the new age because the struggles are dissimilar. Primarily, our parents faced the apartheid, but now we face the economic struggle in the quest of financial freedom. We could change leaders and vote for persons with wings, we could form more than hundred and fifteen political parties, and suggest structural change but there is need for us to realise the reason why Rebekah chooses to change Jacob's clothes not Jacob. Therefore, this rebirth of image will assist the party to be at the forefront with exceeding majority because then it means the agenda pushes goals that are relevant to the needs of the county.

Perhaps Rebekah reminds us a great lesson, that when we have the wheel there is not a single need to re-invent it, why should we create more institutions in our country when we already have so much, Rebekah basically reengineered the existing system.

The Skin of a Goat Kid

HERE REBEKAH—WHO, NOW and again, will be a picture of citizens who support Jacob Zuma as she supported Jacob—did not request the skin of a goat kid, but she strictly said *goat kids*.

The catch is that if Jacob gets a goat kid, he already has found a skin of a goat kid. Therefore, the connotation to the skin of a goat kid is that it is a cover since skin covers our flesh; Rebekah declared her support that if Jacob delivered, she will cover him.

It was a decree to cover Jacob in the same way we saw branches supporting and covering Jacob Zuma with a huge cloud of votes in the 2012 Mangaung after predictions of those who undressed Jacob Zuma through political prophecies.

Where do we get such people

Judicious followers always want to know the direction and the target of their leader. The blind don't want another blind man to lead them; their expectations towards the one who leads them are within the capabilities of any human being.

Direction creates reasonable assurance that, although nothing is ever absolute in this journey, such as we have taken with Jacob Zuma, if our leaders can point direction, then we believe achieving outcomes is only a matter of time because direction alone points out progress.

The first part of Rebekah's instruction deals with the location of the target. The operation was different and so the objects. Abraham had to give a life, just as the special generation of leaders who gave their lives for the freedom of this country. Isaac had to dig wells just as the leadership of former president Thabo Mbeki put Africa on a global map. Jacob had to bring two goats and be supportively coupled to a leader whose mission is to liberate people against the financial struggle. It is through Jacob that we have the first twelve hours of the day and the twelve months in a year, but the hours of the day are twenty-four, and the number of Jacob Zuma's kids seems to approach it. Numbers generally do not lie, but if we argue, do we then forget that around the twelfth hour midday on the twelfth month in 2012, Jacob Zuma won the Mangaung elections, being the twelfth ANC president?

Little did Jacob know how much impact he had composed unto the world. For as long as we live, we use a mirror, but when we are gone and are at home, we shall see face to face and know everything as we are known. But Jacob Zuma is more blessed because we have found major pieces of his fate, though Jacob Zuma knows I am afraid he has seen little, but the quality of persons Jacob Zuma will deploy for his assignments will be loud enough even to the deaf citizen even though ANC is a collective-leadership establishment.

Early one morning, I ran to the shop to buy milk as I was late and thought the elders were truly inconsiderate towards me. When I came back home, I poured the milk in the cup to make tea, but Mom whooped me so hard, and she asked me, "Where did you get it?" I never understood that because I thought *milk is milk*. Now I know very well because that milk couldn't stand the test of hot waters. I could not drink from that cup myself because I risked the quality of milk by taking a shortcut, but such habits also jeopardises the quality of our goal. Nowadays, I am hoping that we will become a nation that is willing to take the right direction in pursuit of quality instead of quantity.

What could have caused some RDP houses to fall by the push of a human shoulder? Only if we all built our country as if we were furnishing our private houses then Jacob Zuma's leadership would achieve greater heights.

Perhaps it is essential to recognize that Jacob found the goat kids at home, so where shall Jacob Zuma find individuals who will help him build this country? If we say South Africa is our home, then it means we must all be ready and available to play our role. I lose sleep if we wait in hope for strangers to build our house. It will take South Africans to build South Africa.

Jacob's Goat Kid

THE SUBSEQUENT PART of the instruction is the specification of the object itself. A goat kid has her own interesting characteristics; hence, it is an archetypal choice.

It was, therefore, essential for Jacob to know *what* to take when he left the house; his mission was running behind time.

A goat kid is known for its *innocence, pureness, energy, and lack of horns* (horns are a sign of self-importance), and these features were prophetic to a set of traits Jacob Zuma's leadership would have to possess in order to become a force to reckon with.

Jacob Acts upon the Mandate

THE ABILITY TO go out and get exactly what was expected of him shows us how Jacob kept his focus, and this positioned him at the tip of his victory. At no point do we hear that he was instructed to come back with hair, but his focus afforded him the secret fruits that always hide within the directives of a mandate.

I have frequently wasted a lot of time, worrying about where I will find everything in order to compete with my contenders. Hitherto, I realise that life is not about competition; it is about completing your assignment on earth.

Focus always suffers tests and arguments, which become reasons why we couldn't do what we were expected to do, so Jacob, like any of us, had his own excuses. His concern was his outer appearance, which resembled the conditions out of his control, but whenever something is out of your control, it is in God's control. Although he addressed this limitation to Rebekah, Rebekah seemed to overlook it, but it is not so. Rebekah was convinced that Jacob would be able to do that which was expected of him, but how is this stance dissimilar to the support of those who believe Jacob Zuma will win and succeed in his assignment?

How Much

REBEKAH'S EMPHASIS ON numbers proves that this specificity encloses a special meaning—the *two* goat kids.

Two goat kids reflects Jacob Zuma's supporters sustaining him for the second term as we saw them during Mangaung with their two fingers up on the air as a sign of his return to office for the second term.

Jacob Zuma's supporters raising their two fingers in the air, just as Rebekah who supported Jacob pushed him for two goat kids.

Speed of Service Delivery

Rebekah took a colossal risk: They lacked resources. The fire had to be started. The two goat kids were to be slaughtered. There was much to do, and each minute was instrumental.

The atmosphere was then filled with a sense of urgency. Though I do not cherish competition, if it brings urgency, then it is fine. Esau came back. Esau must have also felt the sense of urgency because his dad mentioned death.

Clearly, Rebekah's tone must have addressed the urgency of this situation since Jacob gripped the message and quickly went out and came back to deliver as it was expected of him.

This was important—as Jacob would become a leader—to understand that issues around speed of delivery could deter his success. It is so relevant to our country because service delivery has been a prevalent challenge in most areas. Despite the fact that the country has limited resources, I do hope that our way forward will enable the government to identify robust systems and programmes that can augment the pace at which the governments at all levels deliver their services timeously to the people. This incorporates the same approach used during campaigns; it would afford us to be a leading society and getting the advantage to understand the real needs of the people at the level where flawless feedback is reachable fluently.

Change of Tone

Jacob had started wondering, like a man beating up his chest with the side of his fist, "Perhaps I could stop my first fears." A moment of hesitation. It is the fear that comes with waiting for results when you know you have played your part. Rebekah had to fulfil her word, she said she will cover Jacob, the people of South Africa also walked on the streets and said they will vote for President Jacob Zuma and they confidently did. Jacob must wait around as he wondered, in hope that the game will bring forth the required taste, but Rebekah knew what Isaac really wanted, and since we said she is a figure of ministers and public servants, this means Isaac's vision was practical and clear to her in the same way the vision of the government must be clear and enlivening to ministers and public servants.

Anxiety grew in Jacob's heart; he was standing between Isaac, who represents the government of our country, and Rebekah, who represents the followers of Jacob Zuma. Rebekah prepared the food and gave it to Jacob. "Jacob, now take it to your father, a verbatim implication to this can be a picture of discussions that occurs between all leaders in the parliament. President Jacob Zuma has to face the members of the parliament just as Jacob had to face Isaac. Jacob had to take the venison to his father, President Jacob Zuma also, let's say, he has to respond to the questions he is asked, no wonder Isaac later showed his doubts, he lacked confidence that the man in from of him was Esau, but also we saw leaders demonstrating their doubts on President Jacob Zuma's ability to lead South Africa, but just as one could say Rebekah was part of the leadership, then it makes sense that within the same house, some will support President Jacob Zuma and others will not, it is how Isaac chose to support Esau and Rebekah supporting Jacob which defines this painting. What causes Jacob to win this battle is his vast support, but those who argue must think about these many ANC seats in the parliament, Jacob also ended up with Isaac and Rebekah, this made Jacob to secure the majority of seats." I can visualize Rebekah joining her hands so tight and interceding for Jacob by heart, remembering those first steps Jacob took as a toddler. Now he was a man; he must be supported towards the steps of his destiny. The day before yesterday, Jacob Zuma was a minister, and His Excellency walked towards presidency. An MEC in December 1994, the ANC national chairperson, and then the ANC deputy president in December 1997. This is similar to the day Jacob stood before Isaac in pursuit of rulership as he presented the venison to Isaac. These positions Jacob Zuma had taken are not different to the venison Jacob brought to his father.

Now Jacob Zuma has become a greater leader, and therefore, his supporters will support him even more as he takes manly steps marching to his fate.

The pressure and the fear within Jacob could not be articulated, but with so much support behind him, success was predictable.

Rebekah encouraged Jacob, "You can do this, Jacob. Don't you let nervousness get the best of you. When your steps are heavy and the sound of your heartbeat is audible, all things are possible. What if this mission goes wrong? Relax, Jacob, and focus. If you made it in the womb, you will make it here." Not only was Jacob wearing someone else's clothes but this goat hair would soon be itchy on him. But does pain really matter when we have a task ahead?

Jacob said, "Shh, Ma! I am too close to Dad."

"Don't forget to disguise your voice," his mom reminded him. But the desk was getting loaded with more issues, and we know that when we get to this point, everything planned could go worse or better; a mess can be a lesson or a blessing. This is the verge of the end where great victory resides, where an ordinary man's tears flow like rain, but heroes reign. Here one step is a decision of victory or a really bad fall.

Immediately Jacob had to recall his brother's voice: deep, strong, and heavy as it normally was with firstborns. "Oh no! This is completely not me, but this is mine". What do you do when your victory is in the space beyond the sky and the astronomer left his jet in your reach and his suit in your suitcase?

Jacob didn't change who he was. He worked on his tone, and today, leaders often adjust their tone to emphasise the urgency of a particular situation

"Dad, here I am."

"Who are you, my son?" Isaac asked, yet not for many times previously Jacob was ever referred to as the son of Isaac. But this time, he called himself the first son of the house. I pondered earnestly; in one event, Jacob Zuma calmed people to realise that he is here and not going anywhere, but what manner of confidence could this be when Jacob Zuma was going through such a blurred time? Nothing. Jacob Zuma is now telling people who he is, just as Jacob told Isaac.

This is the change of tone. Some of us didn't know Jacob Zuma as a person who could respond in this manner, but wait, what can we learn from this change of tone? Creation groans to be delivered from the bondage of corruption. Though Jacob corruptly changed his tone to steal Esau's blessing, we could accomplish the impossible; we could eradicate corruption if we changed our tone towards it.

Although it rains from the skies to the soil, but also geography discoveries proves that the same fog from the soil makes the cloud and consequently rain, this shows that although the tone at the top is very significant but the community at large and the government should work together to combat corruption.

Jacob Uses God's Name

Isaac's response was a positive mark for the end Jacob earnestly hoped for. The probing response "Are you my son?" was a great impetus for Jacob, realising that, finally, he was being recognised by his own predecessor. Which successor seeks not to hear from his predecessor? The fact that his sonship was being questioned was a confirmation.

Even so, Pilate confirmed my Lord's supremacy when he questioned it in Luke 23:3. "Are you the king of the Jews?" My Lord said, "It is as you say." But Pilate, being a politician, knew that questions were actually answers in politics and, thus, an order in which power and authority of rulership is confirmed. Jacob Zuma also will have to endure others who question his leadership.

This is the home of persecution, an unapproachable ocean to those who are visitors of courage, but a victor has to placate himself while anticipating the end result. King David also encouraged himself in the Lord.

I can imagine Rebekah holding her hands and speaking in sign languages. "Jacob, talk. Talk to him. You are going to have to talk to get this one." But Jacob contemplated the value of this sacrifice, which could cost his life. Rebekah's support was ample to cheer Jacob. Have the followers of Jacob Zuma not done the same in this day? Although the ANC has millions of supporters, but then again, those who campaign during elections will also have the obligation to talk to the voters, so that Isaac can listen and decide on the one who shall take his vote, also President Jacob Zuma will have to talk to the people before he is voted.

"Dad, my name is Esau, your firstborn. I have done as you have instructed me. Arise, I pray you. Sit and eat of my venison so that you may give me your blessing."

Since our spirit is allergic to lies, one would hope Jacob would be afraid to lie in front of his father. But Jacob could not turn back at this stage, so he lied and was called a liar. But even so, when Jacob Zuma answered about his house and said he had a bond, many people said he lied, and consequently, they called him a liar.

Isaac's lack of confidence towards Jacob was ceaselessly glued into his heart. Jacob brought all the evidence to prove he was Esau. The venison was well prepared. Isaac asked Jacob, "But how did you do it so quickly?"

"Because the Lord your God brought it to me." Even a child can tell if this response was true or fallacious. *Did God bring it to you, Jacob?*

Jacob's punctual delivery of the services shocked Isaac and convinced him that Jacob deserved the blessing, but do they not believe that Jacob Zuma deserves the second term of office? They do, but the pace of delivery will be a major component for Jacob Zuma's leadership as it was for Jacob.

Jacob literally used the name of God and said, "God brought it to me." Scholars proved that Jacob's reply was deceptive because he actually went out to get the goat kids; they who are strictly of faith say this was not profanity. It was an assertion of faith, but time will dispense the truth.

The earth has moved for more than two thousand years, and then our clock hits the same point. Jacob Zuma, whose name is Jacob also, said "ANC will rule until the coming of *Jesus Christ*." They argued about this expression, but all I ever witnessed was our-time Jacob using the name of God. This is what Jacob did, and Jacob Zuma did the same thing.

Isaac said to Jacob, "Come near, I pray you, that I may feel you, my son, whether you are my son Esau or not." This plainly proves Isaac's suspicion, for being a wise man as he was, he had seen loads of cases where rulership was robbed. Though he had all this knowledge, his eyes were getting dim. Rebekah's support for Jacob had become a hard force, and though Jacob had the contender, his advantage was his contender's disadvantage. Esau was not so close to Rebekah. Rebekah here represents the public.

Today people around say, "Anyway, if we didn't vote for the man or the ANC, who could we have voted for?" It is this detachment to Rebekah that became Jacob's opportunity. Although some of our leaders are very strong, but the fact that they are seen to be detached to the people, this becomes President Jacob Zuma's opportunity. I could gamble for once in my life, *if* Esau had found Rebekah's support Jacob wouldn't have made it that far, clearly here the people are the secret matrix of success.

In the present day, Jacob Zuma is closer to the people than his opposition, but how is this new? We have seen how Jacob was so close to Rebekah, who supported him all the way through his flaws and father's laws.

Jacob's Emotional Intelligence

IT'S LIKE I lived in that day. I can make up his measured steps, but my gladness is in greater tidings; the steps of a righteous man are ordered by God. Jacob came near his father, and Isaac felt him. "The voice is Jacob's voice, but the hands are Esau's hands." This destructive confusion frustrated the decision of an old man. He did not know when he would fall asleep for good, and this was not the situation he preferred to see, for also his spine had grown feeble. He must make a decision while he could still stand.

Weight and exigency of this matter knocked down Isaac's drained heart. The predicament is the choice, but Jacob's evidence was compelling. Should we follow the voice or the hands that knocked on the door? But the hands are not his, so how can the voice be his? Jacob became two in one, but also can anyone tell me when does a man we have always seen smiling, makes his opponents to fade after a fight. Could this smile be the veil of his strength? The old man opted to employ Jacob's hands for his last vote. I find it strange that such a knowledgeable man would opt for hands over a voice. It is with hands that we knock on the door, but through the voice, we identify identity. Yet Isaac chose to take the sound of the knock and not the voice of the one who knocked.

Apparently, the decision to choose hands was incited by a futurist idea that a man who would lead this country would generally not be a guru in academics. Do we not know that, even up to this day, an innately ordinary man can be more skilled at blue-collar jobs than an educated man?

Jacob lived many years away from his home. Consequently, this disadvantaged him from all that his brother enjoyed, but what could this be in this modern day? It means Jacob missed an opportunity to go to school as he attended to his uncle's flock, but like situations such as that which Jacob Zuma faced in his childhood, this opportunity slipped off the hands of his time.

A speech is a product of a voice despite the fact that, in most cases, it is fashioned by education. Isaac's response proved that Jacob's speech did not meet Esau's speech, this yet proved that in the present day Jacob would have been deprived education, Jacob Zuma also joined the African National Congress at a younger age, at that age I finished matric. When we all look to focus on personal development, Jacob and Jacob Zuma's interest was far from self development. They both are the artefact of the struggle they have faced in their early years. Amidst that, Esau may have been educated and eloquent in this context, but the blessing was looking for a natural plumber, a naturally gifted man, whose hands were skilled for the service. But just so, the people of South Africa also needed a leader whose speech did not have to be so perfect as long as services were performed and delivery was well-timed.

There has been many incidents where Jacob Zuma has been criticised by the words he said, the other time it was about how he reads his speeches, some compared him to former leaders who are perceived to be fluent in their speeches, yesterday there were altered interpretations about Africans and animals when a dog was quoted, but many citizens will still not remove their vote on President Jacob Zuma, although he is discredited and implicated by how people arbitrate his speeches more often than the number of times a man looks at the mirror, even in the beginning Jacob had shortcomings on his voice, it was his natural gift that sealed his fate, but if anyone should say Jacob Zuma is not naturally intelligent then we should argue the existence of the sun in a misty day.

If I consider the aging factor, I could relatively measure the deterioration of Isaac's hearing and sight abilities. They were declining moderately proportional; anyone who cannot see or hear appositely will consequently employ outward conditions to gather enough evidence to make a final decision. The voice, in this case, was such an indispensable component, but rules were modified for a chosen man. Water turns to wine in the time of a chosen man, but some people can only see the picture when the flash is on, but I had no need to zoom some titles of the newspapers on the poles of the streets, for they were titled in capital letters, *the Zuma moment.*

Eventually Isaac felt Jacob. The phrase "he felt him" was prophetic to how people would use their feelings as a major constituent in making a judgement whether to support or not support Jacob Zuma, it appears that there has been a constant subjectivity when people are dealing with Jacob Zuma. No wonder Jacob Zuma faces so much uncomfortable events that could obliterate a man's passion. Isaac felt Jacob, and people feel for Jacob Zuma.

There are people who support Jacob Zuma because they see a victim whose rival lack mercy. On Friday, the twenty-fifth of May 2012, it was reported that Jacob Zuma's lawyer cried in court. This report seems to follow the idea of Jacob Zuma being followed by different emotions. People felt for Jacob Zuma what others lacked in their care.

Nevertheless, here and now, people often confess temper as a great weakness. Even Moses had shortcomings on temper. Hitherto, we have witnessed various opportunities where an ordinary black man will not have allowed a woman to walk over his head, yet His Excellency smiled where strong man could have fallen short of patience.

Your calmness directs and dictates the steps of your opposition

Do I believe that Jacob Zuma is perfect? Only God is perfect! Yet Jacob Zuma's emotional element of his persona has proven his exceptional cerebral calmness. Since people often want to be led by a person whose emotional intelligence is outstanding, this gives Jacob Zuma more followers when he is affronted yet still manages to keep his smile. Since people wonder how much this man can take, they will all end up giving their support as strength until his opponents realise that the more they beat him, they multiply him. I guess that's the way it works with *the Jacobs*.

Exodus 1:12

Some will misread Jacob Zuma's silence as fear, but veterans know very well his stillness. The rich would not have wanted him in their reach. Who could have survived such negativity thrown at him? Some said Jacob Zuma will not survive, but His Excellency handled such disapproval with composure. He has faced impolite and severe condemnation with a smirk. We have not heard of such state where citizens will not regard an image of a president. Surprisingly, everything shall work together for his favour.

Jacob, blamed and sliced with sharp blades, remained meek, and through Jacob Zuma's life, I can measure what Jacob must have faced.

The meek shall inherit the earth.
—Matthew 5:5

The Voice of Jacob

THOUGH THERE ARE a billion words in the vocabulary of each language, the spirit man searches for one voice; it is the voice of God and in the voice, he shall hear the right word.

Abraham was such a busy man, but he heard the voice and said, "Here I am," when God called him. Though Adam sinned, he would not have responded if he heard not the voice. How shall they hear if they do not listen?

A leader who can listen to the needs of his people is what people have sought for; violence will increase where people are not listened to. If we say so, then why did Isaac disregard Jacob's voice? It is because most South African politicians are known for big English words, but people want a leader whose talk is moving towards action.

Talk is cheap

No wonder Isaac opted for Jacob's hands and not a speech that could quake his lexis.

Transparency of National Systems

HANDS GENERALLY HAVE ominous tendencies. Today they bestow tenderness and kindness, but last night, the same hands shed blood of innocent men. Unless a man's hands are clean, then that man will receive a blessing from the Lord and God of righteousness.

This attentive indulgence makes me wonder if Isaac ever thought about the risk that existed in choosing Jacob's hands over his voice, yet I have no muscle to revile his justification to vote for Jacob. I cannot afford the price of such a philosophical transgression. Isaac was convinced by Jacob's *speed of delivery* and not the things Jacob said during his election campaign.

Although Jacob was not the only one knocking on the rulership door, as many usually emerge on the ballot paper during the elections, the elections were but a knock. Those who seek to lead the government will also have to stand before the community in the same way Jacob stood before his father, because the government is not only taken by words but by availability, from that day to the coming hours kingdoms suffer violence and they who take it do so by force. If political party leaders want to govern, they will have to be practically accessible to the people. Jacob came to his father, he spoke to him in, and in force he took the blessing (vote) and consequently took the government in the hands of the eloquent Esau. In the same way Jacob stood before Isaac to convince him that he was the man for the job, just so politicians or presidential candidates also have to stand before the citizens and persuade them for a vote. What is interesting about Jacob's campaign is the set of portfolio evidence Jacob shared with Isaac and since it cannot be argued that the ANC has achieved some milestones, this is type of progress that made Isaac to realise the need to vote for the man in front of him, but also President Jacob Zuma is the man in front of us. The decision to open the door is exclusively a right of each voter. Isaac had the same right. Jacob's key to victory was being the only one available within reach when Isaac—who represents the people—needed someone who would deliver the venison, a version of people's needs.

The instant question is why Isaac chose to feel Jacob's hands; why not legs or shoulders?

Literally, hands are body structures by which we hold, but in this elevated context, this was therefore a shadow of systems of the national government. The cleanliness of Jacob's hands is a representation of transparency of national systems; food prepared by dirty hands is never easy to swallow for a sober man unless he is really hungry. A clean government is more than a need. There is an acceptable amount of optimism also, that the clean audit mandate within the government sectors will purge away the mud that easily entangles on these key structures of the government. Municipalities which have come out clean should be extoled.

Blessed to Be Served

Jacob brought the food, and his father ate. Isaac then blessed (voted for) Jacob. "Let people serve you and nations bow down to you; be the lord over your brethren." If these are the words of Isaac upon Jacob, then what do they really seek upon the life of Jacob Zuma?

Jacob Zuma is followed by the words that were spoken to Jacob; *his cabinet has great public servants.* Jacob became a leader of the nation while Jacob Zuma became the president of the country.

A photo by Gallo Images that shows incisive and highly regarded individuals who have served under the Jacob Zuma leadership. This again proves that Jacob Zuma is blessed to be served by great servants just as Jacob was blessed.

When Esau arrived, Isaac said, "I have eaten before you came and I blessed him." This was a clear indication that Jacob won the fight before he got into the boxing ring, and this was an unbearable embarrassment for Esau. How does it happen? But has it not been so with the elections? Every time we get into the elections, we already know the ANC will win.

These are the steps of Jacob. He won before Esau got into the ring.

Plot Against Jacob

Esau cried out exceedingly and became bitter for the ordeal that seemed unfair, so he comforted himself that he would *kill Jacob*. This would be the only way to regain rulership. Jacob was not aware until his spy, Rebekah, heard the news and counselled him not to take this matter up but flee from his brother's environs.

These were blood brothers; it would be a phony thing to say they never had good times, but it is in good times where a brother confesses his weakness and such information becomes a threat when conflict knocks on the door of disagreement. Jacob was a wise man; he left, but few of us allow rumours to vanish without a brawl. For Jacob, it was even hard because home was the source of all these issues, but home is a place where we are all suppose to find hope. Home is the place where we trust to find shelter, but Jacob found hatred and experienced division in his father's house, and there was a plot against him.

Few days ago, many people thought the plot against Jacob Zuma by his fellow comrades would fashion great enmity. Even so, with the reported plot in Mangaung to overthrow the government, Jacob Zuma kept his cool and somehow moved the public away from this. Inside plots generally crack the walls of any house; instead, the speculations of the plot vanished like a ghost.

This is not new; Jacob Zuma had just turned to a page that Jacob lived when his own brother plotted against him.

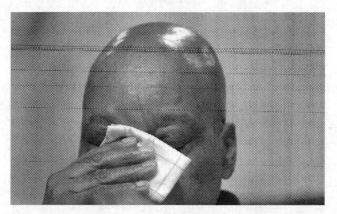

A photo by Gallo Images: Jacob Zuma wipes his sweat like a man who is trying to understand reasons for his conflict.

Accountability

"But where do I go?"

"Jacob, there is a man. Flee to him. Laban is my brother. He is your uncle. Though adversity now tears us apart, your uncle will keep you safe." An imminent fatal fight between two brothers of one house was effortlessly avoided because *there was a man in the gap.*

A man who feared God. A man who would not mistreat or molest Jacob and step on God's toes.

There are a few of us who have had the opportunity of a father-and-son relationship. This literally means the next generation of leaders could be fatherless leaders who have never tasted the sweetness of a father-and-son relationship. While this is a threat for our future leadership, there is an opportunity to strengthen accountability. Of course, South Africans aspire for a leadership that is more accountable than political.

Jacob's stay with his uncle changed him. He reported almost *every* lost goat and paid for it; there would have been no other way to teach him accountability. How Laban, the uncle of Jacob comes into the picture is interesting since the influence of Jacob Zuma's uncle cannot be easily forgotten.

If Jethro, the *uncle* of Moses, was far from reach, Moses would not have learnt accountability, and consequently, Joshua's government would battle with matters of accountability. Therefore, it was necessary that this curtain should be rended *from the top to the bottom*, even so in this epoch.

Jacob Is Elected to Save the Future at Stake

In each incident, communication between Jacob and Rebekah seemed to find a connection. Jacob yet again listened; he went to his uncle. Rebekah prepared the provision for the new trip and promised to wait earnestly to hear what this situation would become so that when Esau's fury dissolves, Rebekah would send a message for Jacob to come back home. This turned out to be a challenge since there were no cell phones then, but also the African National Congress had a challenge trying to mobilise operations from a distance and through other people just as Isaac and Rebekah were using Laban.

The support and comfort Jacob received overcame the fear of embarking on a new journey; it imprinted the importance of home in Jacob's heart. At the same time, Jacob was steadily developing a defence force at home and outside his country. He befriended a friend of the friend of his enemy. Rebekah was close to Isaac just as Isaac was close to Esau, who was Jacob's enemy. It makes it easy to execute a troop when we have friends inside their camp—should I say more, there are *speculations* that some politicians are planted in opposition parties for the mission of the ANC. That may well be a corridor talk, but it is evidenced by beliefs that even Inkatha Freedom Party was the idea of the ANC. It is purported also that Zanele Ka MaGwaza is like an underground mechanism of the ANC.

Rebekah went to Isaac in favour of Jacob. "My lord, you know that I am weary of my life because of the daughters your first son has married." In essence, Rebekah, who represents Jacob Zuma's supporters, is not talking about husband and wife in this context. She is referring to ANC sons who have chosen to unite with other oppositional political parties that have been established by women.

Photo by Gallo Images shows Dr. M. Lekota a former ANC son and Lindiwe Mazibuko, a woman from an oppositional political party. Seemingly joining ideas in a no confidence motion against Jacob Zuma. Esau also chose to marry the women his father warned him not to Marry

This reflection changed the way Isaac looked at Jacob. Now Jacob became a path to a better future. Jacob's decision to marry a daughter who had been raised to honour the faith and tradition of his father would protect the purpose of God. During the end of the 1980s, Jacob Zuma became the head of the ANC Intelligence Department and took this position at a time when the ANC had a complex task of protecting the organisation from infiltration and to ensure its survival. But this is of no difference; Isaac wanted to protect his house through Jacob so that it would survive and not be infiltrated.

Therefore, Jacob's success for future leadership was supported by both his parents because it would secure survival, but could this mean we should learn something from the fact the veterans and Umkhonto we Sizwe members nominated Jacob Zuma? Although the deliberation is composite, Jacob's success for future leadership was based on the rationale that the future would be secured.

Esau's decision to marry these strange women was detrimental to the future because the house would eventually give birth to a confused generation of leaders. As a result, Isaac and Rebekah found it wise to nominate and support Jacob for leadership that would benefit the future.

But here and there, we may need to quote living individuals.

"An ANC stalwart has called President Jacob Zuma the better choice for ANC president." Quoted from The Star Newspaper, September 13 2012. Is it not a bombshell, that these words were quoted as said by former honourable president Thabo Mbeki's mother, yet Jacob's success was also well spoken of by Esau's mother at the time when Esau was a no longer a firstborn since Jacob had taken the birth right, but also these words came out just while Jacob Zuma is the president, which can be directly translated as the firstborn of South Africa in this period. This is too analogous to be inadvertent.

It is amazing because, at this stage, Jacob was awaiting to be blessed for a second time. He received all the support and was blessed. Jacob Zuma also received identical support when he also waited to be voted for the *second term* as Jacob waited to be blessed for the *second time*

Isaac, on the other side, could not suppress the restlessness brought by this situation; he knew how his father took extra miles to save the vision of the house when he found him a wife, and now it was his turn to pay the debts of his offspring.

We have not only received life from our fathers but we have borrowed the purpose of life from our offspring.

The picture of the way forward was becoming vivid to Isaac. That is, to support Jacob." But Isaac could not publicly show his support towards Jacob as some who knew what Jacob had done would consider Isaac's support as an idiotic move, but in essence, Isaac sat behind the scenes and supported Jacob.

Imagine the manner of critics either the Honourable Nelson Mandela or Thabo Mbeki would have to stomach if they publicly showed their support for Jacob Zuma's leadership, but there was nothing wrong with Jacob except that approval would seem to have favourites and be inconsistent. However, this made Jacob to end up with more unseen support, which only manifested when he took over. Should we also wait to see the same result after the 2014 elections even when we know? There are more citizens who vote for ANC, yet they have not or will not publicly show their membership. I reckon Jacobs are made that way; they have more supporters behind the scenes.

Our day is not different to that day. We see so much support results after elections. Even in the 2012 Mangaung, the result outdid the predictions; it is because Jacob Zuma has more followers than those he has seen.

Wait, you will see them marching through the main streets of the cities and roads of the rural places when Jacob Zuma of the ANC has won the next national elections.

Jacob found a blessing and support in the centre of his vicissitudes and grace for a second chance to take apposite resolutions going forward and not only decisions that would benefit him but decisions that would profit the offspring of his nation, who are the future.

Jacob Displays an African Value

"REBEKAH!" I HEAR a shout that was once powerful. With time it has become toothless. It is Isaac. "Where is the younger one?"

"Who? Jacob?"

"Call him. I need to bless him again." This observably happened in the absence of Esau. This seemed to follow the order of politics and backstabbing. What Esau and Isaac did against Jacob was now being done by Jacob, Rebekah, and Isaac against Esau. But we have seen it now and again in politics where the knife turns against the chef as the wheel rolls to the future with lanes of history in its body. Nothing is new. For Jacob, this was a supreme stamp of his future. But as much as the fate of a politician in politics is largely determined by supporters, Jacob's future leadership was determined by the support his parents gave him.

Jacob's respect towards his parents had taken him far beyond where his brains would. Jacob's respect to his parents is just a translation of Jacob Zuma's respect towards the ANC veterans and older political comrades. This is the factor of his persona that works out more goodness in his favour; the nomination for second term by veterans says it all.

Jacob must have thought, I messed up twice and thought my parents would forsake me, but twice he has blessed me. Respect is a penetrating hook of the game.

"Son, we have been together for a long time. I have shown you the way and raised you with care here. You are leaving now, and my legs are tired. My eyes are growing dim.

"I deem not to enforce any more rules upon you. You are a grown man now, but there is one more thing I need from you."

"Does Dad want me to cook?" Although there could have been a concern of what his dad wanted him to do, at this point, he would do anything for his father. He had just been blessed twice, which meant he had already gained *two votes* while his opposition had *one*. But wait, when we see the results of the Mangaung, Jacob Zuma got 2, 986 votes from the delegates. This *two* seems to rematerialize in the life of Jacob Zuma as it constantly appeared in Jacob's life. Furthermore, Jacob was supported by his parents, which reflected his home-based support, and KZN does not wander around but does the same, and Jacob Zuma is nominated and supported without problems.

"Arise. Go as your mother said. Go to the house of Bethuel, your mother's father, and take a wife there from the daughters of Laban, your mother's brother."

The fact that, at this age, Jacob was still hearing from his parents tells us more. Some do suggest that he was a man who tried to please almost everybody around him, but parents only gain such access to kids who show respect. Respect became Jacob's strongest foundation. He wasn't only favoured by God but also those who were around him. Yet in this current day, our-time pharisees have altered the way of truth, but we should remember not to westernise the African seed.

> Now I want you to realize that the head of every man is Christ,
> **and the head of the woman is man**, and the head of Christ is God.
> —1 Corinthians 11:3

I established a point where faith meets African values. Then where is the sting of arrogance? If weird manners are a silhouette of politics, then there is a need for some of us to remain apolitical.

Jacob's respect towards his parents became a giant drive, which also became a strong force to the victory of Jacob Zuma in Mangaung. My generation will learn that respect and honour of parents will attract blessings in the way of the one who is called for a greater destiny.

Our diversity should not turn us to a taciturn country whose shortcoming is debasing African values; respect is an African value.

"May God Almighty bless you, Jacob. May you be fruitful and multiply so that you may become a multitude of people. May he give you the blessing of your grandfather to your descendants so that you may inherit the land in which you are now a stranger." These were the last words from his father, words a bank cannot afford to finance.

Think of it; Isaac said, "Be blessed." Is this not so with Jacob Zuma in the present day if you consider his disadvantaged background? He said, "Be fruitful and become a multitude of people." Nevertheless, which of us here is named Jacob and has lot of offspring whose sons also flourishes except for Jacob Zuma.

Could Jacob Zuma possibly walk upon such good predestination without following its principles? We have seen him suffer, but he kept so much respect for others. Urbane citizens ask me if African values will decrease tax and increase jobs. No! Money buys milk, but African values and beliefs produce the cream in the milk.

Jacob: Away from the Home Country

Jacob's journey to his uncle was not getting any shorter. He travelled alone and consequently learnt to esteem and treat strangers with care. At one stage, he met strangers and called them brothers. Though Jacob Zuma is indicted for brothering diverse folks, and this was quoted as a prediction of his fall, Jacob had done this for the sake of his fate.

The long-distance expedition and struggle to the destination became an excellent training; a novice under extreme conditions where weather changed drastically, his persistence taught him godly statutes in terrifying deserts. The measurement lengthwise of the trip was working out what God constantly worked in the man in him.

He faced lonely nights without a weapon, intimidated by the roar of bears and lions where you barely meet a human being, In a Biography of Jacob Zuma, Jeremy Gordin also questioned how Jacob Zuma coped with not seeing a single face from home. But as I sat (trembling) waiting for the President in MaKhumalo's dining apartment on the 3rd of March 2013, I couldn't figure out how President Jacob Zuma made it without her love, she is as strong as Rebekah, anyway Jacob also, had no one to visit him during this time.

Therefore both these indistinguishable monarchs witnessed God's protection without the help of bodyguards.

> But in that coming day no weapon fashioned against you will succeed.
> —Isaiah 54:7

This was sufficient to revolutionize his focus on his way away from home. A journey to the discovery of self and realisation of what and how people feel when they are in search of their well-being. Extraordinary ways moulded the leader in him so that when the blessing grew exceedingly, he would grow relatively humble.

The journey of Jacob to his uncle is a depiction of Jacob Zuma's period away from South Africa since December 1975 and his years in Southern Africa. But since Jacob stayed with his uncle, it was necessary that Jacob Zuma should stay within the neighbouring countries that could be referred to as brothers of Africa's mother, whose name is South Africa, since Laban was a brother of the mother of Jacob. Southern countries played an epic role during the time of difficulty in South Africa; these countries covered South Africa in the same way Laban covered Jacob. While Isaac's plan was to hoard the plan of God from being polluted by other races, the ANC's plan was survival and to save itself from infiltration.

And therefore, Jacob spent time away from his home country

"Awuleth' Umshin Wam"

Jacob arrived in a certain place and stayed there all night, alone, seeing the approach of the sunset. The heartrending feeling of sleeping in a dark, desolated, and ruthless situation during frightening nights away from home proved that Jacob was meeting reality. No supper, no love, so he took a stone at that place and put it under his head as a pillow.

These are the makings of a great leader; desperate moments reminded him of prayer. Hard times also made Jacob Zuma an exquisite leader. Remarkably, Jacob Zuma could start a song in a funeral. Jacob Zuma can relate to the man whose mansion is a shack, and the people have since looked for a leader whose speech does not only address the rich but can reach the corners of a poor man's shoe and walk with them step by step into the future that changes their life.

Citizens know that miracles won't work; if it were that way, parliament would be full of magicians. People yearn to see their existence in the plans of their government, but how shall a leader change the situation of his people if he hasn't been through what his people have gone through?

At one stage, black people, especially from KZN, were just so excited by Jacob Zuma's origination; people saw their own Barack Obama from Nkandla.

As the dark hour of the night approached, birds began to sing the songs of the sunset. In the morning, a chicken's loudest cry woke everybody up at home; the sun had risen again. What a triumphant day we anticipated! During the day, a dazzling pigeon sang, "Wozani nizobona amabele amdokwe avuthiwe," and we listened to this bird with a smile, for its tune brought joy—a message of hope: "Everything will be okay." But home seemed a trillion miles away for Jacob. A hadida must have cried, but I was born and bred under the care of elders who understood times and meaning from meaningless creatures.

My grandmother said, "When you hear a hadida, go back home." This bird sounded as if it sang a song of misery. Our construal was that it said, "I travelled, had difficulties along the way, but now that it is the rise of sunset, I am going back home." There comes a time when we all want to go back home because home is where we belong. Oh! It must have been a hurting minute for Jacob because it was out of his options, and the night was too close. Jacob was filled with fear and loneliness in a place where *izindonga* echoes every nerve-racking reverberation; *sometimes* it's even much better to fight than to be alone, but Jacob Zuma became Jacob and faced a similar challenge, his ten years in prison says it all. Imagine the experience of being imprisoned for ten years, and the cause has nothing to do with you as a person but it is for the people. Jacob's tough time was also for the generations to come, on the other hand was the struggle of apartheid bore by our fathers, not for us? President Jacob Zuma also took endured a fair share of the apartheid burden which could have been cumbersome to the rest of us today.

Jacob placed the stone under his head and slept, how stones find a way to enter into this account gives our notion more weight, but I do not intend to ponder on the fact that while Jacob Zuma and other prisoners were in prison, they also had to break up stones.

We visited Pietermaritzburg and camped for a weekend. At night, we rolled our clothes and made them pillows, but why does Jacob use a stone as a pillow instead of his clothes?

Biblically, a stone was often used as a weapon. One day, in a certain place, a king whose name was Saul had all kinds of swords, war outfits made of steel, and troops around him. They sat and waited, but Goliath despised them. A boy they despised, but a leader in God's eyes, came through and saw this *uncircumcised man* despising the people of God, for *he looked at them as the armies of God.*

King Saul clothed David with his suit. "But wait," David said. "I can't fight with these. Allow me to go down to pick a few stones." This decision to get stones signifies contemporarily a man taking his *machine gun* before the fight, yet a righteous man's weapon is kneeling *down* in prayer.

The sling, which he used to shoot Goliath, is seen to be a substitute for a modern pistol; it was as swift as a bullet of an AK-47. If we were conversing about David, we could elaborate more on why this shepherd hits the *forehead* of his *opposition.*

Delay with me here; Jacob is about to sleep. He takes a stone, but since he saw that stone as a weapon, I have no doubt, if anything happened in that night, Jacob could have used that stone as a weapon. If it wasn't so, those who had guns would not have placed their guns close to their head when they slept. Basically, Jacob knew that anything could happen during that night. "*Wathi awulethe umshini wami* before I sleep because anything can happen here." In the same way, I fear not to call those days a night because when Jacob Zuma faced hard times, he then sang, "Umshini wami awu wena uyangibambezela."

The Stone on the Head

A SUBSEQUENT DERIVATIVE IMPLICATION of a stone was heard in Ephesus. A man professed our establishment and said, "We are built on the foundation of the apostles and prophets."

Generally, stones were used for building, while the church is also seen as a building. The physical building of the church is also built with stones like a normal building as it is important for a building to have a cornerstone.

Christ, then, being the one who contains and defines the whole doctrine of the Christian church, becomes the cornerstone of the church. He is the integral part of the building, the basis that defines the charter of the church.

A nation that believes in Christ as a cornerstone of its foundations will be established and built by God.

> What then shall we say to these **things**?
> If God be for us who can be against us?
> —Romans 8:31

The true vine was not yet revealed to them, and therefore, their life was like a shadow of a tree, which is the closest thing to the actual tree itself, but we are the branches of the actual tree.

For that reason, a stone was used in reference to the chief cornerstone since the cornerstone takes an important position.

Jacob's decision to take the stone and use it as a pillow for his head was prophetic for the insight of South African leaders. Jacob's head represents the head of the state—the government of the country—and therefore, it would be wise if leaders placed Christ in an important position in the government in order to make it through this night.

Making Christ the head means South Africa would be able *to withstand* not only evil principalities from the kingdom of darkness but also anything that swanks and presents itself in a manner that makes people think God is pathetic or does not exist, such as poverty, job losses, incurable diseases, and crisis of the economy.

Jacob Zuma sang "Awu wena uyangibambezela" because all the talk and accusations were delaying progress; in fear of a war that could materialise, this song was opposed, but Christ cannot be opposed. There is no *better machine gun* than him. Few days passed by, and some prayed and anointed Jacob Zuma. It seemed as if the head of South Africa was considering Christ as a cornerstone for this government.

The Dream of Jacob

Jacob FELL ASLEEP. A ladder was set up on the earth, and the top of it reached heaven. The angels of God, ascending and descending on it. Look, the Lord stood above him and said, "I am the Lord, God of your grandfather and the God of your father. I will give you this land. *You shall spread abroad to the four corners of the earth.* I am with you and will keep you wherever you go. I will not leave you until I have done all that I have spoken to you."

For the fulfilment of the words "four corners of the earth," Jacob Zuma travelled and visited the African countries, Europe, America, and Asia. I am a sitting witness of the fulfilment of words that were set upon Jacob, yet they are settling upon Jacob Zuma.

Jacob nods off, and this awakens him in disbelief. "Word! I am dreaming."

Jacob was still mystified in drowsiness. "Such dreams can only be found where eagles soar, but who am I to have such a dream?" With excitement and fear, he said, "This must be the house of God," because there he found a dream.

Jacob's dream had more unto it than a customary dream of a night. The specificity of the details of his dream is enlivening.

There was a massive number of angels walking, up and down. What is this? This symbolised a million people walking with President

Jacob Zuma, picture the number of South African citizens who support the African National Congress. Furthermore, the fact that angels walked above him displays submission to higher powers and putting people above him.

Then why are they going up and down? It is because the economy of the country follows the same pattern during the leadership of Jacob Zuma.

Why is the ladder from the earth to the heavens? Since heaven is a much better place than here, it was a metaphor of the actual ANC vision, wherein the people of South Africa long to walk from the place of struggle to a palace, a better life for all, for—lo!—the people are the vanguard of the struggle.

Nevertheless, the spiritual atmosphere of leadership now and again seeks a dream, but there is no dream without a man. No wonder the appointed time seeks not to choose people over skills; otherwise, leaders would become bigger than a dream. It is not supposed to be so. Moses was not eloquent in speech; therefore, Aaron made a speech for Moses, but out of the genuineness of his heart to change people's lives, we believe that Moses was a greater leader. Therefore, what happened to Aaron? Nothing, *no servant must be bigger than his master.*

> Every house builder should be smaller than the house
> he is building if he will complete it with ease.

Therefore, this time has picked and appointed its very own, and who am I not to hold Jacob Zuma in the highest regard?

Jacob's dream qualified him for leadership: the elements such as a multitude of angels, the direction from earth to heaven, and the fact that he sees himself below angels proved the end of his pomposity and a birth of a leader who will venerate the people in the struggle.

He had found that igniting passion called a dream. Dreams evoke the past about our future; they are a path with hope. Consequently, because Jacob Zuma also dreamed and led us, he is not really different from Jacob, who dreamt and led Israel.

His dream will stir up not just this generation but also the generations that are yet to be born. They shall know that Jacob Zuma was here. By your walk, you will make a mark. Who thought one of our own had such audacity to dream and go this far? You have broken forth out of what was once a limitation. I hope you are ready to see your inspired reproduction. The switch may be down episodically because of the financial storm and global market fluctuations, but, Mr. President, you have made us believe in ourselves. You have given birth to hope not only to the South Africans who eat *izambane likampondo* but to the cold dwellings *nemikhukhu* of rejected men who are raising their daughters in a one-bedroom shack where life moves from the hand to mouth. These are people who will love to see Jacob Zuma visit their residence even when he is no longer a president.

So when you are feeling down, remember, you are human. When everything you have done so far seems not to shine, don't you forget that you are a national switch. Every detriment that occurs in the parliament should never keep your head down.

You could have chosen to be an ordinary man from the loins of KwaZulu Natal, but your persistence picked the light and consequently broke the psychological umbilical cord that lived from the day when our fathers dug gold but never became gods of riches.

Let us gear on for the next term and make things happen, even at the lowest level; generally, it takes time to build a palace. Yes, we will definitely hit some potholes, like a road to Ngwavuma, but if we keep going, we will get there.

The People of the East

THE MORNING AFTER an awful night finally came, it was time to move on. Jacob packed his possessions and left. Just in a short passageway of his walk, he meets the *people from the land of the east.*

Originally, God had organically scattered people according to the four corners of the earth. The world map proves that we can meet different races if we look specifically on the east corner to identify all people therein, but in this context, who are these people in the life of Jacob Zuma?

The people of the east are the Indian race, a people that Jacob Zuma would meet and befriend. The people of the east played a critical role in the life of Jacob, but have we not heard the same about some Indians in Jacob Zuma's life? In 2005, there were strong reports of Schabir Shaik, who, in this case, is a picture of the Indian race, reported to have supported Jacob Zuma financially before he became the president. But even Jacob, when he met the people of the east, was not a leader of the nation at that time, and therefore, since Jacob met the people of the east, here and there, an Indian face has appeared where there was also an issue about Jacob Zuma.

Yesterday, Vivian Reddy sealed the revelation about the people of the east in Jacob Zuma's life.

There are diverse countries in the Eastern flank of the world map, yet we have seen more from the eastern society flocking into South Africa than any other societies from the world. We barely have a corner without a chap from China or Pakistan, this has much similarity to be drawn and attached to the period when Jacob met the people of the east because that is how they managed to get their way into his country. President Jacob Zuma also attended a ministerial meeting of the forum of China-Africa cooperation which was held in China. Just as Jacob met the people of the east in their country Jacob Zuma met the Chinese people in China. The people of China or at least the east to say have found their way to South Africa, but just as they played a big role in the life of Jacob, it is believed that China is coming to South Africa with prodigious benefits, and so we so saw BRICS and China as part of the nations therein in our midst, all I see is Jacob meeting the people of the east.

Vivian Reddy and President Jacob Zuma—Vivian Reddy appears for the shepherds of the east which Jacob met in his journey.

The Three Groups of Flock

He looked right up; there he saw a well in the field. As he stared, he saw three flocks of sheep by the well. *The flocks were watered out of that well*; a great *stone* was upon the *mouth of the well*. Amazingly, when all the flocks were gathered there, the shepherds rolled the stone from the well's mouth and watered the sheep, and they put the stone back on the well's mouth.

The three groups of flock portray the citizens of South Africa. Since Jacob Zuma is the president, he is also like a shepherd, and the citizens of the republic all are like his flock.

The meaning of *three flocks* proves that people of South Africa cannot afford *the same standard of living*; in effect, like school kids, we can go to the same school, but not the same class. But a leader's vision is extended because his assessment must not be biased to a certain class. Jacob Zuma is the principal of the school, and his administration are the teachers in classes. The three flocks of sheep therefore were prophetic to the categorisation of classes of the economy, indicative of the rich, middle, and the poor.

The shepherds waited on that day; our government officials and national leaders need to wait until the people are gathered together and then be watered. We cannot afford to have egocentric shepherds who feed themselves first then, at times, consider the needs of the people.

If leaders wait until the flock is gathered, the South African government will accomplish equality in the supply of government services, wherein the people are fed with equality and without nepotism through class and race.

The National Planning Commission project must be applauded because it will eliminate inequality and, such, is in line with godliness and human values.

Jacob's One-Minded Leaders

JACOB MET THE shepherds. "My brothers, where are you from?"

"We are from Haran," they said.

"Do you know Laban, the son of Nahor?"

"Well, yes, indeed, we know him."

"Is he well?"

"He is well." Their short responses showed their relentlessness towards Jacob. Who is this guy with so many questions?

Even so some who know Jacob Zuma said he asked many questions during his night hour classes.

Early in the year 2000, I arrived at Empangeni to meet a cousin of mine that I had not seen for almost ten years. We both hoped to recognize each other through our natural instincts, but as he delayed, I introduced myself to a crew of guys and explained to them where I was going. This made it easy for them to give me directions. In almost a similar case, Jacob does the opposite, but I reflected if this was an apposite way to approach strangers in their territory. Now that I have met different people, I find it incredibly intelligent for Jacob to talk to these men in this manner. In the past, we exhausted much time explicating who we are (our purpose) and where we were going (our goal). Hitherto, we established that the people we gave so much time to in workshops and training could still not understand our vision because they were also looking for something else other than what we showed them. We could not be of help to them, and neither could they be of help to us. What a waste of time!

But can we afford to have members who barely recognize the culture of the ANC and its dynamics? Neither am I an expert in that, but I speak as one who brings good tidings.

Jacob's strategy saved him time. "Look," the shepherds said, "not only do we know where you are going but we also come from there. After watering the flock, we will be going there."

This was prophetical to leaders, government officials, servants, and people that Jacob Zuma would find. Leaders who have no agenda other than the one Jacob Zuma has dished onto the cabinet table. The real meaning of this is when we meet people who are of the same mind as we are; people whose speech is twinned to ours. There is a much greater purpose that can be achieved when members of the ANC are united.

Genesis 11:1-8
The Lord came down to see the city and the tower, which the people had built, and the Lord said, "Behold, **they are one people** and **they all have one speech**—one mind; this is only the beginning of what they can do but nothing they ever imagine will be impossible for them to do."

But the Lord will scatter them who are driven by pursuit of personal glory.

People-First-Based Leadership

In practice, a shepherd possesses the traits of modern-day leadership. The shepherd walks in front of the sheep; he finds and leads the flock to greener pastures. Some shepherds carry a rod and use it to bring back the sheep that are going astray; this rod is a representation of a fair and balanced justice system.

Other shepherds carry a staff. A remarkable part of the staff is its end where it bends. That part is used frequently when a sheep falls into a pit. With it, a shepherd pulls the sheep out of the pit, and I would think of this as adequate national financial systems, infrastructure and resources that pull citizens out of the financial pit the country is facing; nevertheless, the staff brings hope.

> Thy rod and staff—they comfort me.
> —Psalms 23:4

When a sheep sees a rod or a staff, it knows that the protector has come, so everything will be okay. Can South Africans say the same about their government?

Jacob was naturally transformational; he remained restless with environments he couldn't revolutionize. "Brothers, look at the time. Can't we take the sheep into their pasture since the sun is still too high?"

"No, here we don't do that, Jacob. We water the flock." This portrays leadership which considers people first.

Finally, Jacob met people who shared his vision, people with the same speech as his, but they are a group of folks who will stand their ground and follow the right principles. "Here we roll the stone from the well's mouth and water the sheep."

Jacob was a wise man, not that he didn't mean what he said to the shepherds; he was used to saying one thing meaning the other. He was trying to shift them from their responsibility so that if they should do that, they would unconsciously take him to his uncle. But Jacob learnt an important lesson, a lesson of selflessness where the agenda prioritises people. Since there was supposed to be a link, selflessness became an integral value of the ANC.

Jacob learnt adaptation and ways to manage issues that arose from a diversity of people where principles could not be transformed to suit personal goals. He recognised leadership that addressed the needs of the sheep (people) first. In one speech, Jacob Zuma said that taking leadership in government is not an opportunity for self-enrichment.

Jacob Meets Her

"Jacob? Look, that is Laban's daughter [Rachel]. She is coming with her father's sheep," the shepherds said.

"Is it?" With a strange face, Jacob looked at her. Gentleman where I come from, it is a man who pastures the sheep, but this was a different woman. She was different from all the girls Jacob met back at home. A woman with leadership traits, one who could not be caged by domestic responsibilities, she also took care of the issues of her father's house. But how can we align this presentation to this era?

She personifies a woman that has knowledge of global issues, an outdoor woman who has male servants, and not only a professional woman but an African leader. Could this be a predestined personification of Nkosazana Dlamini Zuma? Even before I was born, Nkosazana Dlamini-Zuma took a trip to Tanzania during 1982? Is it not strange that Rachel met Jacob on her trip to the wells? Taking the sheep to be watered, but also Nkosazana Dlamini-Zuma's trip to Tanzania would later benefit the people of South Africa. Look at this, between Jacob and Rachel there were *four children* (even though the other two came through Bilhal, Rachel's maid) and here comes Msholozi, Gugu, Nokuthula and Nomonde, *are they not four* in this day between President Jacob Zuma and Nkosazana Dlamini-Zuma?

As they were busy talking, she approached with her father's sheep. Quickly Jacob ran to the position of the shepherds and rolled the stone from the mouth of the well and watered the flock that Rachel had brought to them for watering. "Who is this nameless gentleman, servants?" Could Rachel be charmed? If so, it means we are getting more correct DNA results between Jacob and Jacob Zuma because Jacob Zuma is also known for his charms. Jacob kissed Rachel, and she lifted up her voice. She is so not used to men who start their conversations with a kiss or charms. She wept and ran back home.

Most people have interpreted the term holy kiss to hugging.
President Jacob Zuma hugs Nkosazana Dlamini Zuma.

She is the pride of decent women who uphold high morals though they sit in prominent leadership positions. She was taught to run away with her innocence and virginity in the city of sin, where girls are infatuated by expensive cars. She cares for the sheep, she is a businesswoman, and she's just been kissed by Jacob.

She is a shepherdess, and Jacob is a shepherd—this becomes a similar trait they share. A shepherdess Jacob Zuma met before he became the president of the country. Even Jacob met Rachel before he became a shepherd.

Jacob and Polygamy

RACHEL RAN AND told her father that she had met a relative. "Dad, he kissed me." He must be the son of Rebekah, and this was great news to Uncle Laban. "Where is my nephew?" Laban ran to meet him; he embraced and hugged him. "Let's go to the house. We shall blather more when we get there." And Jacob got a chance to finally open up his chest which was full of success and stories of personal failure. He told Laban everything, and their comradeship grew even stronger.

While he served Laban as a shepherd or as the president of the sheep, he found himself more than one wife; thus, he became a polygamist. But this happened prophetically because Jacob Zuma would do the same at the time when he served the country in the same way Jacob served Laban. Jacob Zuma served as the president of the Republic of South Africa in the same way Jacob served Laban, in the same order of Jacob. Jacob Zuma found himself more favour because whoever finds a wife finds favour from Jehovah.

Proverbs 18:22
Jacob became a polygamist

Back then from the beginning, the kings of our faith have practiced polygamy, some who denied it ended up in bed with their maidservants, remember Abraham? But if you take a closer look at men who were polygamist you will certainly pick up wisdom and bravery, remember Solomon? Although people seek to find what errors come out of it, but polygamy is a gift that can only be afforded by the most perceptive and rational individuals, for it requires skill beyond love, nevertheless Like Jacob, His Excellency became a polygamist and I am not ashamed to mention Jacob as one of the kings of our faith. Some will ask if I condone polygamy, but my motivation here is the bravery, His Excellency President Jacob Zuma has displayed and thus becoming a genuine custodian of our culture and traditions.

The Honourable President Jacob G Zuma with his lovely wives.

Reuben Has Mandrakes

Jacob begot many sons, as many as twelve, and they grew mightily.

The firstborn was Reuben, who went out at the time of *wheat harvest* and found *mandrakes* in the *field*. He brought them to his mother, Leah, but Rachel begged Leah for the mandrakes.

Winnie Madikizela Mandela kisses Julius Malema, like a mother kissing her son. Leah first refused to give out Reuben's Mandrakes. We could confidently say she protected Reuben in the same way, many accused Julius Malema for causing chaos, Winnie Madikizela Mandela was seen displaying motherly protection towards Julius Malema.

The meaning of the wheat harvest is the time of advantage, a time that could have been used unequivocally by the ANC to gain even more leads.

Mandrakes were since used as a love plant, but nowadays, this is misconstrued. Through time, we have learnt that what was used constructively is now used for the opposite. Mandrakes were used to build relationships, but easily, the purpose has been distorted.

Here we find one of Jacob's sons; could this denote a biological son? Not all the time, a son be a successor or a strong follower. Reuben was the older son—a leader of all the other sons. Jacob's sons give a depiction of the Youth League because this is generally where ANC sons are primed. Then who is Reuben? Who could this prophecy manifest through, and what could be the implication of mandrakes? We have seen the elders of the ANC reprimanding the youth league, this modification of leadership in the Youth League is parallel to Reuben's circumstances, he had all chances to be a successor, but his conduct became the detriment of his success. Gwede Mantashe was quoted saying *"We can't have instant leadership, the difference between filter coffee and instant coffee is quality"*

A picture of Julius Malema, former ANC YL leader, the picture portrays a man who is asking if it could be him who brought the chaos, as referred to in this context, against Jacob Zuma. Reuben brought mandrakes

The connotation towards Reuben coming back home with mandrakes was symbolic to a young leader whose etiquettes changed against his leader. Originally, his strength and acumen had been used to erect greater purposes for the house of Jacob, but with time, we have seen change.

Reuben's mandrakes unsettled the entire house and brought disrepute. Eventually the mandrakes were used against Jacob; but some members in the parliament charged Jacob Zuma for Julius Malema's actions. Reuben was a leader of all the other sons.

Yesterday an electricity supply element in the geyser was bungled, so we replaced the old elements with new ones. As I opened the shower, I almost got burnt. I reduced water and effortlessly pushed the tap to the left so that water would be warm; it remained hot until I radically pushed it to the far left. This showed me how dangerous an inquisitive mind of a youth can be if there is no one to subject it under control. The geyser should give us warm water and not burn us with hot water. How do we keep this situation under control? I controlled the tap.

In this case, the geyser signifies a mind of any youth; these new electric elements typify powerful support and backup. The tap is his power; the tap will only need redirection if we hope to benefit from the geyser.

Jacob kept quiet, and the young man was not regimented for coming back with mandrakes *at a time of wheat harvest*. But Reuben is the son of the house, and there could be a rescue plan for the fruits of the house that have fallen by the wayside.

The most powerful thing in a fruit is the seed it carries more than its taste, especially since taste can be distorted by conditions.

But since we are mentally limitless we cannot be caged by political connotations or ideology of this revelation, the citizens of South Africa should be captivated to join hands with the government in the fight against drugs. Reuben came home with mandrakes and therefore parents must be the first line of defence against this difficultly crushing our youth, principally the born-frees. Mr President, the projects and streets of our residences are full of drugs.

Women's Great Role in Leadership

Leah bore a baby girl, a flower among thorns, whose delicacy sat beneath a massive defence, and she was named Dinah. Just after Dinah was born, Rachel was no longer barren; she bore a son and called him *Joseph*.

Joseph was the last-born, who profited from more attention than most of his brothers because his parents had grown old, and he had a sister who raised him so well. He was raised under the leadership of a sister. As a result, Joseph did not only learn how to use his father's mistakes to attain perfection but he understood women because he grew under a lady's care that raised a man out of the boy.

The other nine boys had lived without a sister. This nonexistence of a woman symbolised the existing problem of sexism and gender disrespect in our country. Yet the birth of Joseph after his sister is a clear indication of what Jacob's successor will fully achieve—a non-sexist and non-racial country.

At one stage, Joseph escaped a queen who wanted him in bed so bad, but the juvenile leader was not raised by a nanny; he was raised by a lady! This proved woman's role in the life of leaders. Women have played an important role in the life of great leaders. When Pharaoh killed all baby boys, fearing strong oppositional and future leadership, Moses landed in the hands of a woman who was Pharaoh's daughter.

I have discovered much significance of women in the life of highly regarded leaders; leaders have a woman moment in their lives where the mission is only made possible by a woman.

When women are born, leaders are borne.

I am comforted to see women in leading positions; this demonstrates how Jacob Zuma has not crushed women under his feet. Women now have sufficient chances to change Africa for the better.

Photo by Gallo Images. Ms. Baleka Mbete is one of the South African women who hold a high position and has played an important role in the leadership of the country.

Photo by Gallo Images. Ms. Nkosazana Dlamini-Zuma, a South African woman who holds a high position and has played a vital role in the leadership of the country.

Jacob's Journey Back to Nkandla

JACOB'S FAMILY WAS finally happy and cherished him because of his achievements. In my conversation with Sbonelo Zuma (one of Jacob Zuma's sons), I picked up how much Jacob Zuma is cherished. In one statement, he said, "At home, Dad is the father, not a president." But Jacob had personally lived his life and survived different and dissenting environments. Though his experience made him wise, his soul was growing weary; all he ever wanted then was to move back to *his native soil*.

He begged his uncle, but Laban would not let him go peacefully.

Jacob had finally realised a need to put much focus on his homeland in order to share and give back through the blessing of God upon his life, and since Jacob did this, I have been watching almost all the year-ends in Nkandla. President Jacob Zuma's home slaughters cows and welcomes people; this can never exceed the definition of Jacob's willingness to share his blessing with his homeland.

Our era has gloomy pieces though; an old woman is deserted, so she depends and provide for her grandchildren through pension. I saw her son's mansion in Sandton. Her dedicated efforts of waking up and selling mielie meal in winter have been forgotten.

Money that a former miner could have spent for a personal gift is spared for his daughter who studies medicine. In autumn, he coughs to fatality, but his countless letters to his daughter, who has become a doctor, finds no response. How soon have we forgotten where we came from?

I believe we are born into particular communities for a purpose; that's why we can choose friends, but we can't choose family. Part of the purpose is to give back. People often seek a target for blame, yet each community has its own successful individuals, professionals, and the rest who have settled in Hillcrest. The inescapable summer rains from heaven will ruin the oven because an old man's house is roofless. Are we failed by the government, or have we failed ourselves?

I thought there would be more socially responsible citizens by now who take pride in their originations. Citizens willing to sponsor disadvantaged former schools where kids still go to with holes in their shoes, where we have a vision without regarding television as an intention. Nowadays, people in the city are more into publicity; they sponsor multiracial and private schools and expand developed roads, but some kids haven't seen a desktop on their desk.

As it was, it shall be. Laban had no thought of Jacob's originations, and he stood against Jacob's plan, which would flourish the homeland of Jacob.

Perhaps the improvement of the Inkandla property and its road will create questions to alarmed taxpayers because our facts are from the media, but until all critics shift the development of urban areas to rural areas, developments seen in Inkandla will continue to reserve thoughtfulness and demonstrate to the youth an African leader who regards his originations. People have questioned if leaders and celebrities ever think of their parents and originations.

Do I encourage *ogimbela kwesabo* (self-interested leaders)? No! I am a socially responsible citizen whose seedful grape shall fall in the soil of Vryheid and become manure for the generations to come, but we also have learnt such goodness from Jacob Zuma.

Since Jacob's decision was to bless his native soil, how is it different from the Inkandla development, where Jacob Zuma was born? Amazingly, these developments happened while Jacob Zuma is still the president just as Jacob was still the leader when he decided to do so.

A photo by Gallo Images that shows road development in Nkandla. Kids from school walking a long distance

The Spotted and Black Sheep

Jacob FED THE flock for the last time and passed through it that day; he removed all the *spotted* animals and all the *black* ones.

Jacob worked his years as a representation of Jacob Zuma's terms of office; the two seven years within which Jacob married his wives represent two terms in which also Jacob married his wives. Jacob pastured the flock and ultimately discovered tricks of the flock other shepherds knew not.

One day, he took away all the spotted and black animals, but this arrangement and division was too creative to be ignored.

The Spotted Sheep

The spotted animals are people around Jacob Zuma whose conduct brings a desire to sniff. There will be a desire for services of Thuli Madonsela. Jacob's decision to remove the spotted sheep was not nice but very wise to convey a plain message of what sheep he was looking for around him; the sheep are a reflection of their leader.

Jacob removed the spotted sheep just as Jacob Zuma reshuffled his cabinet members. In shock, we all were, but I presume Jacob Zuma had seen spots. Jacob Zuma announced a major cabinet reshuffle and appointed new ministers and deputy ministers to improve and accelerate service delivery in the country when the government needed to ascertain what worked and what needed to be changed or strengthened. How is this different from Jacob's intention to remove the underproductive animals around him?

Here and there also, there have been *spots* in deployment of cadres lacking meticulous expertise to vital positions. This has consequently seemed to affect service delivery, but removing these sheep would be like an implementation of rigorous procedures for employment and appointment policies that will have a positive effect on the pace of those goals that Jacob Zuma's administration seeks to achieve even at the lowest levels.

The Black Sheep

Significantly, Jacob made Joseph a coat of many colours. This coat and its many colours are a contemporary representation of the diversity of races in South Africa. It perfectly illustrates our rainbow flag, a flag of many colours.

Jacob's resolution to remove the black sheep was a lucid clue of Jacob Zuma's mission among the black people. Blacks have found a leader who would practically remove them from financial struggle for their progression. But wait, that's not the end; Jacob Zuma walked on this prophecy when he showed his sense of care for all races and genders by employing a generational blend in his cabinet.

If you will read Genesis after this and wonder why Jacob placed a rod between the animals, the rationale is plain: a rod was also used repeatedly for punishment. Jacob Zuma's decision to reshuffle his cabinet was of no difference because it is not pleasant to lose your job. Left and right, we saw some ministers losing their jobs.

Further, Jacob peeled white streaks in the rods, and white appeared as it was still *hidden* in the rods. It seems that the black sheep could not see what was in the rods, but Jacob peeled it so that they could see the agenda surreptitiously concealed in the rods. The rods are people whose intention is division in the country through colour and racial discrimination issues.

This became a prophetic admission of racial discrimination and intolerance that has existed through hidden agendas, but if we are afraid to admit racism in South Africa, we are guilty as one who said he has no sin.

Effect of Wages to the Economy

THE SCRIPTURE LABELLED the removing of spotted sheep as a manifestation of all the hidden spots—concealed unjust acts Laban committed against Jacob. The Bible said Laban actually robbed Jacob of his wages; yet again, after so much blame the sons of Laban shoved upon Jacob, they did not know that Jacob had been deprived. This taught Jacob an important lesson: leaders must be aware that treatment of workers and wages can affect their leadership.

It can become a negative disorder to the economic downfall. We have had a downbeat mark to the economy because of the strikes arising from concerns of wages and salaries from miners and farmers; some already have to choose between buying bread and paying the taxi fare. The price of a dollar to a rand has reached almost R9.00 during the early end of 2012; the last time it traded above this was in the last recession. Employers must take necessary precautions. Yes, there are erstwhile international factors contributing to the tension of our economy, but an ordinary house has a defence mechanism with which it is able to preserve itself during the time when the global economic wall suffers cracks.

God has instructed masters, bosses, and farmers to be fair to their servants and treat them well; I believe that citizens at all levels are key to economic recovery.

Behold, any wages of the labourers who have reaped in your fields, which you have fraudulently withheld from them, cry out against you; and the cries of those who have laboured have entered into the ears of the Lord of hosts.

—James 5:4

Challenged by Brother

THE SONS OF Laban were vexed towards Jacob; having lost trust in him, they got together and made claims that Jacob took their father's flock, and therefore, he must be cut out. These claims that Jacob used or took their father's flock to enrich himself are not dissimilar to the claims that Jacob Zuma used state money to build his house. The fact that they gathered together to prove their distrust and loss of confidence is a visual reproduction of the day when some gathered against Jacob Zuma and tabled a debate for a vote of no confidence. Jacob's innocent response is comparable to Jacob Zuma's reply when he said, *"People are talking without knowing, saying I have used the state money. I have not done so."*

Laban turned bitter towards Jacob. Even a guilty bloke cannot suffer a cold dish. Jacob was hurt by this, but Jacob Zuma is also human. The frustrations and claims brought by Laban's sons made Jacob Zuma irritably respond to the claims brought to him.

Consequently, this hostility left Jacob with no one to trust; where he found friendship, now he found opposition. It happens when the tap gives both sour and sweet waters. Laban, *who would once kill* for Jacob, turned bitter against him. At home, things were not so good; his brother became his rival. This is similar to what we witnessed when some members who were once in Zuma's camp in 2007 turned out later to be his rivals in 2012.

In the midst of such perplexity, God confirmed and stamped the move back home, for this is where he would find much support. Even so, when the elections of the president for the second term approached, it seemed that our Jacob, who goes by the name of Jacob Zuma, gained more support from his homeland, KwaZulu Natal.

If you have to think about what Jacob went through on his way to his uncle, you will feel the pain and lonesome feelings, but now, he had gained flock, the sheep, the camels and the goats etc., just as President Jacob Zuma has gained not only wealth but countless supporters. The journey was going to be even tougher; throwing the towel would mean he had no care for people on his shoulders.

This trying time forced Jacob to go back home and make peace with his brother. But wait, Rebekah hadn't sent a signal for Jacob, and this was a weakness in the decision to move forward. Some spread the news that Jacob Zuma's decision to step forward for presidency had such a form of weakness since some of his followers' stands were vague, but this is the same form of Laban's changed stance towards Jacob. What could have changed this special relationship? Some say there are no eternal friends in politics.

If Jacob chose to rely on his intellect, there were too many evident factors that proved that Esau would stand against him. Esau had also grown and gained vast support, but this would be the time they meet as challengers, a brother-to-brother challenge.

This then brings a picture of the 2012 Mangaung in which Jacob Zuma saw his political brother, Kgalema Motlanthe, becoming his challenger. In the same way Esau had gained hundreds of soldiers who supported him, the former ANC deputy president also gained support of hundreds of votes.

It is the toughest option we have to take. Practically, people want to invest when the markets are secure, but God had declared to be his security, Jacob had taken a step of faith, because never has it been easier to be challenged by your brother, someone who knows your ins and out, but also Deputy Kgalema Motlante and former president Thabo Mbeki have both sat with President Jacob Zuma many times. If you take a step back home; He will take a step into your opponent's territory. Individuals you never thought would run to you will follow you if you trust God over people.

Cursed is the man whose trust is upon other men.
—Jeremiah 17: 5

Jacob called an urgent meeting, but the only mature supporters were the four women around him.

The *four women* around Jacob represent the four wives of Jacob Zuma. Jacob gained more support from women.

A photo by Gallo Images. The photo shows the four wives of Jacob Zuma (Bongi Ngema, Thobeka Madiba, Nompumelelo Ntuli, and Sizakele Khumalo) sitting in the front row of the ANC meeting almost in the manner in which Jacob's wives sat during the meeting when he had to face Esau.

Jacob's support from his wives made me understand why Jacob Zuma has gained more support from women. Even the Women's league nominated him for the second term.

A photo by Gallo Images shows women from the Women League,
women who have backed Jacob Zuma just as Rebekah backed Jacob.

The following day, Jacob rose up and set everybody for one direction, a direction pointed by him alone.

Jacob's Charges

JACOB LEFT UNEXPECTEDLY without telling Laban, who left to shear his sheep. Isn't it outrageous to hear that such a respected man who once had so much, plus his sons, was now shearing his sheep? This proved Jacob to be a skilled president or shepherd of the sheep beyond Laban's sons who blamed him. When Jacob was gone, they were supposed to be the ones who sheared the sheep but flopped. Since Laban, who was a chief executive took operational duties, we hardly hear of such, but we wait to see the wonders that shall be performed by every Jacob Zuma critic.

On the third day, news came out that Jacob had fled. Laban looked for Jacob, but for *seven days*, they could not find him. They overtook him in the hills of the country. These seven days are a representation of a fairly accurate number of years some have been looking for Jacob Zuma so that charges could be laid against him.

Jacob's team went to meet Laban and company. They claimed that Jacob stole their gods and took their daughters with a sword.

Arms Deal

The use of the word *swords* is prophetical to the case of arms deal. Jacob was alleged to have used swords to gain control. The swords were therefore a foreshadowing of what the generation of this era will witness in their own Jacob, and there was a case of arms deals and Jacob Zuma's name. It seems that Laban later withdrew this charge against Jacob.

Rape Trial

The taking of daughters by sword literally means forcing a woman, but this is nothing other than rape. Yet not long ago, we heard also that Jacob Zuma was facing charges of rape. Jacob was acquitted on this charge, Jacob Zuma was also declared not guilty after the rape trial

Corruption Charges

The inference to the use of gods in this background doesn't literally denote that gods can be stolen. The human-crafted gods were made by gold, and we know that, even to this day, gold is an expensive commodity. Jacob was being accused of corruption, and therefore, charges of corruption were also laid against Jacob Zuma.

Jacob only did not know that one of his own was guilty since Rachel had stolen the golden gods, Jacob Zuma was also associated closely to Shabir Shaik. In the middle of nowhere Rachel advocated Jacob's innocence, the relationship between this new evidence to prove Jacob innocent could be twinned to the response of Vivian Reddy on payments of Jacob Zuma's house in Nkandla.

Laban's hunt and search of gold gods in Jacob's house is an imagery of a modern investigation, but nothing was found, and *Jacob was acquitted*. It is remarkable to note that Laban charged Jacob first without investigating him, many people also argued that Jacob Zuma was not getting a fair trial, Zwelinzima Vavi and Blade Nzimande were some among many who backed Jacob Zuma during this testing time.

Jacob experienced a hard time when his opposition followed him to his house even though he had left Laban's house, many people thought of it strange that Jacob Zuma would be followed even to his own house. What Jacob faced, Jacob Zuma faced in the day when the leader of an oppositional party, DA, went to Nkandla. People felt that Jacob Zuma was being followed even to his house. Is it not because Laban followed Jacob?

When Jacob was acquitted, it was a breathe giving moment for his supporters; it removed the weight that delayed their progress. But have we not been delayed by these allegations? This is why many citizens implore that we also quickly get into this phase where all allegations find one end either way because progress is delayed when focus is shifted even slightly.

Support from a Higher Leader

JACOB'S FEARS WERE inwardly growing; nevertheless, he could not turn back anymore. The journey was long, most of his sons were still young, and there was another emerging fight that could occur when he meets his brother, and his sons knew not about this fight. His persistence paid off; the angels of God met him. Angels are basically servants of the highest leader. Jacob had now obtained even more favour when he received the support of a higher leader in front of his sons. It served not only as a great spiritual boost as it would equally be, politically, if a higher leader proved his support publicly for a leader, but it was important for his sons and followers to witness their father's backup.

There is no greater moment in life than when
your predecessor is approved by his predecessor in
front of people.

In essence, it is like winning a vote of those leaders
who came before you

It drastically changed the way his sons perceived him; he gained a lot of respect because, finally, his sons did not only get a chance to see him as a leader but they met the leader who was advising their leader. There is a point where we all are servants, where accountability and submission of a leader to his highest authorities and predecessors are more than certification of leadership.

Jacob's Strength of Humility

T HE SUPPORT AND credit from the servants of a higher leader made Jacob regain his confidence; quickly, he used it for his advantage and sent messengers before him to meet his brother. "Tell him *his servant* sent you. Tell him that I pray I may find favour in his eyes." When the messengers returned to Jacob, they told him that Esau was coming to meet him with four hundred men. Jacob was greatly distressed; he divided his people into two companies so that if Esau should come to wipe him out, one company would survive.

Being so frightened, Jacob remained humble and strategic, and there can be no greater strength we shall see in this life except from a man who is strong but humble. Arrogance, insensitivity, and war are signs of a man whose heart is full of fear. This intensifying fight proves it all. If his brother finished him, a remnant of his sons would fight because he divided them into groups.

Jacob ended up with many companies that were under the control of his sons, yet here and there, people say Duduzane and Khulubuse are two of Jacob Zuma's sons and business managers because he has given them charge over his companies.

Photo by Gallo Images. Duduzane Zuma is one of Jacob Zuma's sons known for his executive role in some companies. He is a highly regarded and intelligent young man whom the public have said is in charge of Jacob Zuma's companies in the same way the sons of Jacob were in charge of his companies.

*Khulubuse, a man who is highly regarded and considered rich but also
one whom the public have said is in charge of Jacob Zuma's business
in the same way the sons of Jacob were in charge of his companies.*

Jacob's message to his brother demonstrates his realisation on
his strength of *humility*. At this phase, the phrase "his servant" is
unquestionably fallacious because Jacob was bigger and stronger than
his brother, but such humility is stronger than a muscle. It humiliates
those who throw dishonour at you. Even a taxi driver whose agenda is
transporting passengers who are going to the market will step out of
the taxi against pictures that debase his president.

This is the dynamism of Jacob Zuma's humility. Some despised
and rejected him such that much sorrow looked for him, and strong

men hid their faces against his wounds, and some wanted to turn to unknown ways. But again, the rod and staff of the country are placed in his hands. This nation shall learn through your afflictions that if a man will maintain humility, he will gain much for himself and grow up tenderly like a watered plant out of dry ground.

Why did Jacob suddenly regard himself as a servant when he needed to go back home? Not far from yesterday, Jacob Zuma heaped praises to Thabo Mbeki. Jacob Zuma spoke as a servant and regarded Thabo Mbeki as true patriot and a perfectly trained cadre, but this was not strange because I have seen Jacob in this position on the day when he regarded himself as a servant of his brother. Jacob Zuma, further, was addressing a large crowd at the Sauer Park Stadium in Aliwal North in the Eastern Cape. Wait a minute, is this not where Thabo Mbeki hails from? It is not strange that Jacob heaped praises for Esau in Esau's territory. Analysts said Jacob Zuma did this to win the support of the Eastern Cape Province.

Jacob Zuma also hailed Mbeki as a committed ANC cadre, leader, friend, and brother. Before Jacob Zuma started his address, he led the crowd in singing "Somlandela uMbeki yonke indawo," which means "We shall follow Mbeki everywhere he goes." Again how is this singing different from the time when Jacob bowed down before Esau?

Misalignment in One Body

Another night came. Jacob was no longer alone; he was now a family man. He prayed, and everybody lodged there that night. Jacob had become a prayerful husband, father, and leader. His spirit anticipated a fight during that night. That night also represents the night when Jacob Zuma supporters were in wait of the result of Mangaung. Although there was hope that Jacob Zuma would win, somehow, there was a cause of concern because Kgalema Motlanthe had also grown his support in the same way Esau grew his support. Imagining what manner of army his brother was coming up with, while everybody was asleep, he woke up and made everybody cross over the brook until he was left alone in the middle of the night.

Jacob woke up and prayed. When your heart is broken down, rise up and pray *Msholozi*.

Jacob had spent some nights alone, dejected and rejected. On this particular night, a certain man wrestled with him. When the man saw that he did not prevail against Jacob, he touched the hollow of Jacob's thigh, and the hollow of his thigh was misaligned while they wrestled. This misalignment of the thigh characterizes possible division and fracture that could have occurred on the night when Jacob Zuma's victory for president of ANC was announced. No wonder on the nineteenth of December 2012, a major focus of Jacob Zuma's message was unity. Jacob Zuma was realigning the possible misalignment on the ANC thigh.

Your Name Is Not Jacob

"LET ME GO. Let me off, Jacob! The day breaks now," the man said.

"I will not let you go unless you bless me."

"What is your name?"

"Jacob," Jacob responded.

This question was incredibly relevant. At one stage, Jacob had said he was Esau, his parents called him Jacob, and his brother called him a subtle liar and a deceiver, and some called him a polygamist, but *who was Jacob really?*

"You shall no longer be called Jacob, but Israel." But shall one man be a symbol of the whole nation? Jacob became a leader of a nation and therefore was confronted on the subject of the people.

Jacob became a leader of Israel, and Jacob Zuma, whose name is Jacob, became the honourable president of the republic.

The sun shined. Look, Jacob was limping, and this puzzled his *sons* because the old man walked so well yesterday, but now, he walked differently. But this was a metaphor for a leader whose lifestyle will change to suit the manner of his calling. Leadership itself is a high calling.

Jacob and Motlanthe Hug

Jacob raised his eyes and looked. There, his rival was approaching, and it was no lie; he had four hundred men, and this sounds like the hundreds of votes of Kgalema Motlanthe. The steps of such a multitude was bloodcurdling; brave men marching towards Jacob, their noise moved the ground, and the heartbeat soon exceeded the normal pace. In Bloemfontein, the house was also divided, at first, into two groups. The competitive singing and clapping of deputy president Kgalema Motlante's supporters during the Mangaung was bounteous to counsel the hearts of Jacob Zuma's supporters.

Jacob went ahead of his people and bowed himself to the ground, but this was prophetic to the manner in which the opposition would choose to attack Jacob Zuma as an individual, but Esau ran to meet him, and hugged him.

A photo by Gallo Images. The photo shows Jacob Zuma and Kgalema Motlanthe (in the same way Esau hugged his brother when Jacob was returning home) as Jacob Zuma was retaining his ANC presidential seat.

Esau then said, "Brother, let us take our journey and go." But Jacob refused.

Esau's intention to walk head to head with Jacob depicts 13 December 2012, when Kgalema Motlanthe accepted the nomination to challenge Jacob Zuma for presidency.

No to Violence Against Women

Now, DINAH WAS the daughter of the house. She went out to visit other girls as it was habitual that a young girl longed to play with other girls and have all the humorous talks.

A man named Shechem, the *prince* of the country, saw Dinah, took her, lay with her, and defiled her. It was not supposed to be that way. Shechem cunningly used his title and popularity to entice the young girl. A modern connotation to the word *prince* means that Shechem would be an influential and popular man. Even to this day, a prince is a popular man.

I encourage popular and wealthy men to use their muscular influence for the protection of young girls. Situations where old, rich, and famous men lay with young girls should not be promoted in South Africa.

We certainly cannot have men in South Africa who do not esteem women, Jacob's resolution to talk to Shechem's father proved that he took the matter seriously, but also President Jacob Zuma launched the campaign and visited the school, this ascertained that the President took the matter seriously as if his owner daughter had been raped and killed. The President was quoted saying "no woman or child should be beaten, raped, stabbed, shot or attacked in any manner anywhere in our country, whether by known or known attackers". A similar stance

Jacob could have taken, the fact that he allowed his sons to take up the matter, gives an idea of a type of campaign that would be ran by his sons. The campaign has been launched by the Honourable President, now the sons of Africa must demonstrate their determination to restore respect towards women.

I also wish to commend the initiatives and efforts of the government in support of the sixteen days of activism against abuse of women. These initiatives are in line with godliness.

Reconciliation

SHECHEM'S FATHER MET Jacob to discuss the lobola negotiations.

His sons responded, "Your son has deceitfully defiled Dinah, our sister. We will not get into this business with you, for you know not where we come from. It is a disgrace for us to give our sister to an *uncircumcised man* who does not respect our women." The men, who are violent against women, are unmistakably mentally uncircumcised. So Shechem could not postpone circumcision for all his men when they heard that circumcision would get them this precious young girl.

Women should not feel vulnerable or unattended just because the least of sound men are worried about their businesses and profits, we should reminisce that Jacob could have taken the lobola negotiations as a commercial transaction like some men who abuse the traditions of our culture, but he attended to the rape of his daughter meticulously. Though in a majority of times when God was about to change the nation and helped it to progress, He looked for a family and in each generation he called and chose a *man who belonged in a* family, this attested that change begins with us, men, but also we should not ignore that we belong to families, and if we should accomplish restoration against this bug in the family order, we could untangle such troubles as rape and violence against women. This will not only solve the current moral glitches but it will drop the number of street kids in the streets of the beloved South African cities.

The primary impression from the proposal of circumcision sounds as if it neglects rape, but they missed the importance of reconciliation and thought trade and the share of profits would expunge deliberate inattention to rules.

I grew up in Vryheid, where we ran away when we saw a white man's kid, and I still cannot easily overlook that because we cannot disregard that we reside in a country that has mixed and diverse races. Therefore, racial issues will be inherent. But now, we are gearing for a better country, and reconciliation will be a great key for the doors ahead.

Our blood is red, even if it were not so, but black and white always makes the best uniform.

Circumcision

As we page through the years of the kings of faith, we turn to a divergent page. It would be untrue to say the men in the era of Moses were completely not concerned about their families, but the continuing battle was taking a toll on them. As a result, their attention was steadily being dragged out to their family matters. But it is also so today; only the form of battle has changed.

The distance to Canaan from Egypt was detrimental to the love they had for their destiny, and men got tired along the way. The strain of battles did not only affect fathers but sons were gradually losing the meaning of their traditions as a result of their dad's tremendously demanding daily schedule. A man in shopping precincts will remember what colour of socks to buy, but he will forget that his kids are growing psychologically and emotionally just as they are physically, and for that, he needs to be there with them and for them.

As a result of battles, the generation of Moses could not circumcise every man, but we have seen Reuben coming back with mandrakes, and this proves as much that needs have changed, and there is a need to enhance the means to the solution; thus, Jacob's sons pushed Shechem for circumcision.

When circumcision is performed, an elder is there to share his experience and to comfort the young men when they bleed.

In doing this, circumcision embodies mentorship. But since I was hoping to make such recommendation through my perception of circumcision, I actually stood up with the Mangaung delegates to applaud Kgalema Motlanthe for taking up such a call to head the ANC political school. This will deracinate unspeakable manners at the right stage.

This mentorship trail will coach the young and vibrant generation of leaders while they explore the meaning of life and leadership, and such problems could never have been healed by a medical prescription. But the need for political mentors and mentorship cannot be measured; it is equivalent to the presence of the elder during the time that the young men are circumcised. This will break off the umbilical cord that generates a breed of bleeding leaders.

On that note, I extol the government campaign together with the Department of Health to promote male circumcision to outwit probable chances of HIV because, apart from all the depth and meanings here, circumcision is in line with the Bible.

Control of Authority

WHILE SHECHEM AND his team were still in pain from circumcision, two of the sons of Jacob took their swords and came boldly into the city, heeded Hamor and Shechem, and killed all the males who were there.

It was necessary for Jacob to sit down with them and correct them as his sons. This discipline would help them understand how to control public masses. They had done well to stand for what was right, which was to protect Dinah, but they had stopped the flames with fuel.

During August 2012, we witnessed also the sons of the state against the sons of our motherland, but flames cannot be stopped with fuel. Nevertheless, in memory of all the souls lost in Marikana, may their souls rest in peace. I hope that a circumstance such as this one will not befall us again in South Africa; a positive country as ours has no room to cater to negative international attention.

This had happened while Jacob was a leader as it is also occurring during the time in which Jacob Zuma is a leader of the country. I trust that His Excellency, related and relevant structures of the country will work together proactively in the future to remedy and prevent such a tearing incident.

The succeeding meaning of the beheading of Shechem and his crew is clear, Dinah's brothers were livid and could not accept such act, but also some South African's of the affected families might take laws into their hands as Dinah's brothers did, although this is understandable, it is not commendable. The literal *beheading* of Shechem then displays openly that certain people will urge the *capital punishment* for the individuals who have committed hostile crimes. I believe that our flight has already jetted off to their skies. We cannot afford to go back to the first round of the fight. We come a long way. This is the time to rediscover Ubuntu and show the next generation of children that where we come from, our forefathers had no wrist watch, but they could tell what time it was.

Jacob Repositions Himself

A MASSACRE HIS sons had caused—this would surely result into a big political debate about his leadership, but now, Jacob was no more a man of arguments. At this stage, he only lived to protect the future, and the future was his sons, the people who would succeed after his leadership.

A Successor is the fate of a leader

Jacob went back to Bethel and settled there. Remember, Bethel is the same place where he met God while he fled from his brother. The decision to go back to the same place showed that Jacob had learnt how repositioning himself would be a paramount strategy for the intensifying confrontation.

It's been a few years; I used to be a soccer player. My team was losing a goal down, but when the opposition scored the second goal, our coach stood up and said five words that have remained, even audible, to this day. It's as if I chewed a tiny marble, for my body shivered, and so did my hair.

"GET BACK TO YOUR POSITION!"

Nobody asked anybody what that meant or whom it was meant for, but the field became a tin because each of us went back to his position. It is the way we positioned ourselves that petrified the opposition, giving us further permission to long-lasting ball possession. If we want to keep up, we might need to relook at how we have positioned ourselves and the organisation of the people. By the way, this was the first game I played where we ever managed to come back from behind and still win the game in front of a majority of spectators who had written us off.

The house of Jacob repositioned itself because the opposition was gaining momentum through the errors of the sons of the house, but have we also not given some of our members to the opposition?

I believe there is also a forever-existing reason why the ANC needs to constantly be in a position and take on an image that is relevant to the needs of this age, a society whose goals are aligned with the needs of the people.

You Are Who and What God Says You Are

GOD THEN SPOKE to Jacob, *"Your name is not Jacob,* therefore, you shall no longer be called Jacob." But again, who among us really calls Jacob Zuma, Jacob? Don't we always also try to find a respectable name for him when he is around us? It could be by reason of the fact that he is the president of the country. But again, God changed Jacob's name.

"Your name will be Israel, but Israel is a nation." Is it possible that the omniperfect, omnipotent, and omniscient God had forgotten what he said? It is impossible for God to err; the question then is if this is a repetition. The nation was getting ready for the next phase, which necessitated Jacob to be reminded who he really was. Not that he knew not his name, but the noise, the patronisation, and the insults he had dealt with had taken a toll on his identity. But many people will agree that Jacob Zuma has faced the same. After all has been said and done, we have power to put a full stop and start a new sentence that says, "I am who and what God says I am, not what people think, say, and do against me."

A photo by Gallo Images. It depicts Jacob Zuma in the crowd and confusion. His face largely dominates the photo because his life is not about what others say about him; it is who and what God says he is.

Modern organisations frequently accentuate their vision when recruiting a new breed of employees. It is also important for us and our organisation to remember why we ever existed, and consider our revolutionary mission in order to put the needs of the people first. Our existence should not be redefined neither by any circumstance nor by people.

Effectively, God walked with Jacob from the place where he spoke to him. He will walk with you step by step, pit to pit, and though we want to quit when the times are tough and the journey mounts up like Kilimanjaro, it will get better as we revisit our purpose of existence, because that is who and what God says we are.

Death of a Leader

As they journeyed, a loud lamentation went up from the earth to the sky. It disturbed Jacob's eardrum. "What's wrong?" Rachel was in labour. "Hold me! Hold me!"

The sting of labour pains was on her, and this was uncommon. I found out that, at most, labour pains don't remain the same as a woman continues to give birth to her successive kids. At this moment, the opposite happened. Is this an alarm for the heartbreaking pain that Jacob Zuma and South Africa are about to suffer?

The midwife, which represents a group of specialist doctors, ran to her. "Do not fear, Rachel. You shall have this son also." Though she tried to hold on, the pain was unbearable. Her veins became visible as they turned thick and green. Unyielding tears continuously flowed down, passing the pores of her cheeks without pause. A soul Jacob cherished so much was finally departing.

For some strange reason, she called him Benoni, but we also have our own. This Benoni meant that the newborn was the son of sorrow, but for us, it can only be a compass of direction to find out where this death will occur. Benoni is under the province of Gauteng. Jacob called him Benjamin, the son of his *right hand*.

Jacob and Rachel were a couple who had almost always seen eye to eye, but in this moment, their views found different directions.

The first view is represented by a group of citizens who make a circumstantial conclusion, people whose views are obstructed by pain and hardship. As a result, they think South Africa is the worse place to live in. They see this financial bend as an end. Whatever problems the country is currently facing, they think recovery is impossible.

Impossible is a word!

The second group says, "South Africa is Benjamin." Benjamin is the last born as South Africa is the last and bottom country geographically found in Africa. Therefore, we shall rise above all the African countries, for the fact that Benjamin was born after so much pain. Nevertheless, his life is known for uniting the house of Israel. Therefore, also, South Africa shall unite after such a dire loss of a great leader. I personally have no love for such time or chapter in this letter. If I should erase it, though, it means my purpose is self-gratification and honour from people, but I write so that we may also be ready and comforted.

We know they say this country is dead; the politics are dirty, and the conditions will never heal because its systems are self-centred, but we don't see it that way. We believe that together we can make that change we want to see. If we voted a holy angel, we would have still incurred the cost of maintaining his white outfit and that of his cabinet members, and surely, some would table that for debate.

Rachel died!

Who is our modern Rachel?

Rachel is a revelation for this generation, a leader who gave birth to a vision, a leader who sustained Jacob Zuma during his difficult times.

A leader who placed his life on the line for the sake of the vision of country; this is an idea he lived for and would die for.

Since death means separation or discontinuation of a special connection, could Rachel's death be a prophetical portrait of Jacob Zuma's separation with Ms. Nkosazana Dlamini-Zuma? Could it be about the tragic death of Kate Mantsho Zuma? I am afraid to stick to these ideas because the spirit man has no sexual category and mortality. Neither she nor he exists in him; thus, the connotation of the usage of *she* varies now and again. It may often refer to a man whose mind is a womb of visions. If this is so, who could be this most important leader in the life of Jacob Zuma? So we wait for the fulfilment of these shadowy pictures because we are not troubled in the waiting exercise. We have done so for the second coming of Christ, which has gone disputable to the mouths of many, but we wait patiently for many years, without falling in fear. From London to New York, the entire world wants to know the preparations of the South African government when this day shall come. Although we should not refuse the reality and gift of life, that it begins and ends but it is unspeakable for the children to start talking to the neighbours about the death of their father while he is still alive. Nonetheless this is a moment for the sons of the house to stand together because the church is praying for the *Abraham of our time.*

We have a hope of glory in the day of trial and tribulation, and this is the day that paid Jacob a visit; his faith was tested. The people whom he loved were also leaving earth in his face; his father also passed away.

We can't set our fist against a mist; we can only pick up the pieces and make peace with this loss. It has been a great blessing to call such a great global leader as one of ours.

The people Jacob trusted most were about to betray him. Sex between his family and servants was reported, and these issues began to interfere with his leadership image. It just got tougher.

Pain, humiliation, and betrayal were the keys of the song. Yet these are the punches a warrior must take. Now, I speak of Jacob. Although I watched from a distance because my connections could not reach Jacob Zuma for a unique symposium, I saw the years of His Excellency becoming a portrait of Jacob's life.

Sorrow indubitably seemed to be winning, but Joseph was growing.

There is hope for this nation.

Joseph Has a Dream

WE HIT UPON great similarities between Jacob and Joseph, the predecessor and his successor. Joseph was an *indoor man*, occasionally *sent* to check on his brothers. At seventeen, he started *feeding the flock* as his father did when he stayed with his uncle. Jacob's heart grew fond of Joseph.

The interesting clues about who Jacob Zuma's Joseph could be are the traits of Joseph. Joseph was betrayed by his brothers and sold to their enemies. Somehow, later, he makes friends with them, yet in this period, while he becomes a ghost in politics, he becomes a wealthy man, a governor in Egypt. Do I want to advocate Cyril Ramaphosa's return through this ideology? Certainly not! But these similarities need no spectacles. Even so, when I speak of Joseph, I have also fears about him. It is how Pharaoh, who represents the hand of the people who once oppressed our forefathers, loves him, but I speak of Joseph. There also Dinah was born before the leader named Joseph was born and here people tip Nkosazana Dlamini Zuma as the woman who might take over after Jacob Zuma. Here is a foreshadow of the end of this sagacity, Dinah, was the first women born in the house of Jacob, this is the reason why the first women to take over the leadership of South Africa, if it should come to pass in this manner, also would be coming out of the house of Jacob, Jacob Zuma. Nkosazana Dlamini-Zuma is a name and surnames with fulfilment of a purpose.

Further, Joseph made his return while Jacob was still in power, which made me wonder if we could be so in point that Cyril Ramaphosa—who has turned out to be dearest in many people's heart—also makes his clear political return during the time while Jacob Zuma is still in power. Do we want to forget that, at that stage, Joseph was rich beyond measure and the house of Israel was facing a famine? How is it that Cyril Ramaphosa makes his arrival during the time when South Africa is also facing an economical predicament and he is also considered as a seriously wealthy businessman following the likes of Patrice Motsepe.

Anyway, Jacob then made him a *coat of many colours,* and even more, the coat brightened Joseph. This coat of many colours wasn't just colour blocking; it was a reflection of strong international *relationships* that would turn out to be his focus and a solution for the nation during the time of his leadership. The way outsiders esteemed Joseph extend the path of my understanding—do people realize how much confident interest our neighbouring and overseas countries exhibit over Cyril Ramaphosa? He is also tipped to be the successor of President Jacob Zuma or Nkosazana Dlamini-Zuma, yet Joseph was also the successor of Jacob after Dinah was born, this is the T-junction of my vision.

But Joseph didn't know that what happened to Jacob would also happen to him. His brothers also hated him and spoke not peaceably towards him. The tendencies of politics.

Now Joseph had a dream, and when he told them, they hated him even more. But Jacob patiently pondered on the matter, for he had gained much experience in politics and leadership to empower his successor. One looks at the time Jacob Zuma has spent in politics, he will be a relevant predecessor to his successor.

Jacob Zuma Appoints His Successor

Jacob had seen almost all his sons taking their paths. Some had followed the example of his brother and *married strange women*. A thousand miles away, an intelligent business charmer became more famous in the absence of Jacob. He was well-favoured by God but also hated by enemies, yet he grew exceedingly.

This is the day Jacob had seen happening through the eyes of his predecessor; now it had paid him a visit. In the same way, Jacob Zuma will not forever be a president. A man who was once strong and was considered a champion when young men fought with *izinduku* will grow old and grey. All that Jacob wanted to see at this age was to cease the occurrence of a fight that seemed to be generational whenever power had to be handed over by a predecessor to the successor.

When Joseph heard that his father, Jacob, was sick, quickly he took his sons to meet their grandfather, but Jacob strengthened himself when he heard that Joseph was coming. He crafted that habitual lie of parents and predecessors: he gave a word of life for the safety of his successors. Although he was in a dire situation, he acted as if he was not dying; he acted strong for the courage of his successor but also many citizens were wondering if Jacob Zuma was not trying to strengthen the nation when he said Madiba was responding well to the medication

"Son, it's been a long journey. God appeared to me and blessed me in a land where I had no expectation of his visit. Though I had no time to take you through, be humble. God will see you through."

This is a final and realistic conversation, not only between a leader and successor but a father and a son, a relationship that often breaks when a successor has to take over. But Jacob was too wise, and he became nice, and Joseph had more respect for Jacob than he ever had, and this became a turning point for Jacob. He became even greater for welcoming Joseph, whom his brothers had chased away.

Jacob stretched out his right hand and laid it upon the head of Joseph's younger son. Now it was Jacob's turn to nominate and vote for the succeeding leader and, therefore, crossed his hands as we normally cross a vote next to the face of the leader we prefer.

He placed his left hand upon the elder son's head; Joseph tried to correct him, thinking that the old man was insane, but predestination is the end where life begins. Julius Malema and Fikile Mbalula in a few instances were seen to be correcting President Jacob Zuma, I see Joseph trying to shift Jacob's hands. Joseph was displeased—won't you leave it, Joseph? This caused tension between the two. There is a need for us to admit that there will also be problems between Jacob Zuma and his successor, but greatness is too close to be clouded by petty issues. Joseph was displeased; many people say they saw Julius Malema as a future president at the start. Joseph handled his frustrations cautiously, for the matter itself was delicate, as it could have devastated his relationship with Jacob, whatsoever materialized concerning Julius Malema and the President, only rivals adored it, nonetheless there is an endlessly emergent need for Joseph to realize that the relationship he has built with Jacob is momentous to the achievement of his objectives, every so often relationships are the path to accomplish our objectives.

God had chosen a man that once looked weak; he chose a man people could not have chosen years ago because God looks not at man as people do but he looks at the heart. Who could have guessed that

Cyril Ramaphosa would make this come back at this time, at once all the sons including Reuben were forever present before Jacob.

> But the Lord said, "Do not look on his appearance or
> on the height of his stature, because I have rejected him.
> For the Lord sees not as man sees: man looks on the outward
> appearance, but the Lord looks on the heart."
> —1 Samuel 16:7

He blessed Joseph and gave him facts on how God fed him all his life. This conversation was something that Jacob had been deprived of just as the end in Polokwane seemed to be unfriendly, but greatness is doing the opposite of what others did against you. Thus Jacob sat with Joseph in his office and told him about each file and dangerous corner of his journey. Now we have a few predecessors who are willing to sit with their successors, but if we seek a definition for a moment of greatness, this is the cause.

Without this, many fatherless sons or leaderless leaders spend almost a quarter of their lives trying to understand the fishing rod, but we can stop mending and wielding this wild plant in our leadership and politics if we launch an unending relationship between those who take up rulership and those who leave the boxing ring.

Jacob and Joseph faced some differences in the closing meeting; at one stage, Joseph was displeased with Jacob. This continuously acknowledges the reality of problems during the handing-over process. Isaac and Ishmael had problems; Jacob and Esau saw this problem, and in 2007, South Africa witnessed it. It is part of the last meeting, but Jacob's peaceful handing over to his successor made him a legend. It will forever be a benchmark for any leadership at its closing stages. It is not easy to deal with this final chapter, but victory knocks on the doors of those leaders who want to bless their successors with pure hearts before giving up rulership. This door must be closed with dignity.

Jacob Gathers Them All
Babize Bonke Nxamalala

CALLING A MEETING and giving directives wasn't going to be hard for Jacob; he had done this before when he was leaving his uncle. He called an urgent meeting, which turned out to be successful, it was good that Jacob called now all of them, because it would not have sounded good to know that he only had a meeting with Joseph, perhaps they thought this meeting was intended to update them, yet in fact to seal the deal. Could this be the reason why we saw a new set of the National Executive Committee in 2012? The interesting thing to note is that Jacob included almost everyone in the meeting, but many people questioned the inclusion of some leaders in the National Executive Committee, saying Jacob Zuma is trying to protect himself. All I see is Jacob calling them all.

Chronically, heirs and successors often long to know who will be next to take the seat of rulership, but it was crucial for Jacob to show them the way forward, command them, and structure them on their lifestyles and passions. This eliminates the chances of chaos, for if they have to decide the next leader, there could be a needless fight for power. That being said, everything would be determined by how Jacob exits rulership, how Jacob will end his term of office.

Jacob gathered all of them and spoke to them. Although he didn't nominate Joseph since that could have proven him as a biased, autocratic, and dictatorial leader, the last meeting made it clear that Joseph was the one to lead if they were going to be loyal in selecting a leadership that will achieve great heights and dominance even upon the territories of their opposition. Now I earnestly await 2018 and beyond to enjoy the fruits of Jacob Zuma's fate because, if by any chance his handover should match Jacob's exit in rulership, then we would have stepped into greater victory than we ever did when we won the elections.

The set of six photos are by Gallo Images and ANC Media Pix. The photos show a few out of many great leaders, a list of individuals who are strong ANC sons that Jacob would have met if he were in this era. Mr. Zweli Mkhize, Mr. Gwede Mantashe, Julius Malema, Tokyo Sexwale, Thabo Mbeki, Mr. Cyril Ramaphosa, Kgalema Motlanthe, Mathews Phosa, and the man himself, President Jacob Zuma.

The Seat of Legends

WHEN JACOB FINISHED talking to them, he charged them to bury him where his grandfather and father were buried, so his sons purchased the field and the tomb, and they buried him where his grandfather and father were buried.

Jacob's instruction to be buried near his father's grave appeared to others as an act of ancestral worship, but are some of us not strictly devoted to our traditions and culture? Consequently, some will express their gratitude towards God through their ancestors. Yet above all is this desire in Jacob to be with his ancestors. Jacob Zuma also sang songs that honoured the fathers of the ANC such as "Inde lendlela esiyihambayo," "Washo uMandela kubalandeli bakhe," and "Somlandela uLuthuli lapho eya khona." If one gathers all these pieces, our puzzle finds its direction, Jacob Zuma was honouring his political ancestors.

Jacob's emphasis on his message focused on his forefathers and uniting his sons through the last meeting, just as Jacob Zuma's speech and songs in Mangaung seemed to appreciate his political predecessors and so the selection of the members of the National Executive Committee displayed eagerness to achieve unity.

But we who are spiritual have a flawless indulgence to the connotation "buried onto the same location with his grandfather and father." Grandfather Abraham was respected even when he was no more, but do we not highly regard the Honourable Nelson Mandela even though he is no longer a president?

The inclination to be buried with his forefathers signified Jacob's keenness to be realised and given identical reverence after the end of his rulership. It is a characterisation of a position that leaders welcome when they are no longer sitting on the main seat—the honorary president.

Jacob had made his mark and served his generation with an open heart; leaving the main seat made him a greater leader. Even when we pray to this day, we say *God of Jacob*. For his acumen to leave leadership structures in perfect order, conditions will never be perfect.

Nevertheless, never has it ever been so easy before then for everyone to bow before a new leader until Jacob made it easy for Joseph. I wish I had more words, but if my lord should find balance and step into this divinity, he will discover a greater seat than the chair of a president, because this is a preview or the most microscopic portrait of prominence for which His Excellency, President Jacob Zuma was predestined for.

Nxamalala, Msholozi, Mdlovu, Mafahleni

I feel as if, if I continued, I would burn this meat. Though I am facing the ground, with my feet here I wrote, this is my idea to the questions of this era. Finally, I am content with bringing an idea that can contend successfully with the contentions of our fate. I write to you, His Excellency, the Honourable President of the Republic for which I am part of its public and to those whom the arm of understanding may be revealed.

My lord, you once were a subjected man where rent was due and men still didn't know what to do because every bank turned its back against them.

I write to you, Jacob Zuma, because Jacob has continued to appear in your mirror every time I heard about you. I believe that you are a chosen person, a royal leader. In times past, my parents were far from voting tolls, but now we have a chance to make our land a better place. If we overcame the freedom struggle, surely we can overcome the current socioeconomic struggle.

Your efforts, in holistic view and continuous persistence deserve commendation. For it is good to do well so that you may silence Ignorance. I am convinced that he who has started the good work through you will be able to finish it.

Imagine a finished product, South Africa as a fully developed country. Picture a South Africa with equality, with sufficient jobs for its citizens, no poverty, no crime or corruption, and no racial discrimination but access to proper safety and health, and good education systems. I don't mean to give a portrait of heaven, but surely we can make our country a better place. Disputes that say, realistically, my views are impossible could be valid, but here, I have requested people to imagine from Mangaung to major wins. If we can imagine it, we can measure it; if we can measure it, then we can make it.

I look back and make out if this revelation could ever be a total lie, but I am comforted by my familiarities. Never did we liken an elephant against an ant when I grew up, for we always deliberated that an elephant's step could crush an ant without difficulty. Therefore, I am convinced that we also have conceived greatness since Jacob was a man God highly rated and used to construct foundations and structures of the everlasting house. Have I equated His Excellency, President Jacob Zuma to the magnitude of that greatness? Indeed.

In 2009 while I stayed in Victoria Embankment, which is now known as Margret Mqadi. I noticed that I was facing the mirror, the mirror moved to the left and right, but I was raised to cast even bully demons, yet for a minute I thought I should take a careful look at the mirror again and see what this could be, we have heard people saying they have seen ghosts I hoped to see one. What shocked me most was to see myself moving in the mirror while physically I was sitting on the couch. No, it is not a ghost! It is me, I reckoned. But the mirror moved because it was being blown by the wind coming from the open window. The man on the mirror did nothing bigger than what I do all days. He moved to the left and to the right in the order of the movements of the mirror, I pondered thereafter in reality, "can I move to the left or the right"? Before I answered myself I stood up and the man in the mirror also stood up, at first it was him who showed me what I could do while I was sitting, by the way he showed me what I could but that which I was not doing yet, I figured out that this is why the size of greatness that lies within us is incomparable to greatness we show every day. The abilities of the man in the mirror were within my power, and since I grasped that, then I dictated his next moves, I waited not for him to show me again what I could do, I showed him what to do. I learned that he wouldn't have moved in the mirror if there were no winds, I guess somehow what makes us better may initially makes us bitter. The persecuting winds of life are never a good thing but look at how they have made us indestructible.

Jacob was blessed yet he was deprived many times, he was human after all, he made mistakes. Some rated him as a weak patriarch whom God chose and used, but how possible can a house be strong if the foundation and bricks therein are weak?

The paramount definition of Jacob's greatness begins in his twofold name; this makes people to love him while some equally hate him. In general problems were conceived because of his personal choices not within the boundaries of his leadership capacity. He is known for his adroitness and slyness; through his humble attitude he gained advantage over those who were stronger than him. He is a man who valued the fight more than victory to the point that he used his weakness and secondary position to defeat the will of strong patriarchs, his tenacity produced his success.

I fell in love with his loyalty towards his mission even before he became the president or should I say the leader of the nation. Yes, his character does not illustrate the virtual honesty of his grandfather, people argue that Jacob Zuma is so different from Grandfather— Nelson Mandela, this is how some do not regard Jacob as a model, and he is pointed as one noticeably imperfect leader, but God asked Adam—Who told you that you are naked?", because no amount of truth from enemies is ever true, the truth gives light not by its nature by its very source.

Do people overlook that Jacob pulled the house out from infiltration? His struggles have been forgotten, this is becoming common, but his passion and sufferings placed him indisputably at the rank of his forefathers. His polite spirit and imperishable hunger to recoup and consign power into the hands of his race attains complete praise, though some argue that he is not chronologically a legend. His life is a heroic poetry, so much so that what could have never been built was completed because of his earlier life choices and decision to avail himself for the struggle of nation and literally Jacob became an artefact of the struggle. From whichever point I analysed him, I just thought I was thinking about Jacob Zuma, but since Jacob was worshipped by the generations that came after him maybe we are in the same situation, since prophets are hardly celebrated at their homes, then great patriarchs will also be honoured and revered by generations they shall not see.

Since there was transformation, God raised an average man to a greater position for a grander purpose, a mere shepherd became a leader of a nation and the name Jacob to the national designation, therefore I could not shy away but embrace the necessity for our dearly cherished President, Dear Jacob Zuma to meet Jacob at this time. This is the purpose, for which I have sacrificed my nights, and thought sincerity and liberalism could buy us all a light with acceptable watts but also if we should find out what is it exactly that lives in our names.

Yours faithfully,
Sabelo "Soweto" Mandlanzi. A proud South African citizen